Harsh and Lovely Land

Tom Marshall

Harsh and Lovely Land

The Major Canadian Poets
and the Making of a Canadian Tradition

UNIVERSITY OF BRITISH COLUMBIA PRESS
VANCOUVER

HARSH AND LOVELY LAND
The Major Canadian Poets
and the Making of a Canadian Tradition

© The University of British Columbia 1979
Reprinted 1980

CAMROSE LUTHERAN COLLEGE
LIBRARY

Canadian Cataloguing in Publication Data
Marshall, Tom, 1938-
    Harsh and lovely land

    Includes index.
    ISBN 0-7748-0107-7

    1. Canadian poetry (English)—History
and criticism.   2. Poets, Canadian.
I. Title
~~PS8141.M37~~   C811'.009   C79-091007-1
PR9190.2.M37

International Standard Book Numbers:
Hard cover edition: 0-7748-0107-7
Paper cover edition: 0-7748-0130-1

Printed in Canada

for George Woodcock

CONTENTS

ACKNOWLEDGEMENTS

I am grateful to the Canada Council for a grant that enabled me to begin work on this book in 1974-75. Earlier versions of certain parts of the book have been published in the *Canadian Forum*, *Canadian Literature*, the *Malahat Review*, and the *Ontario Review*.

INTRODUCTION

Ralph Gustafson writes (in his Foreword to the revised edition of *The Penguin Book of Canadian Verse*) that "the Canadian occupation is distinguished and distinguishable." It is the purpose of the present book to examine the major Canadian poets and the making of a "distinguished and distinguishable" poetic tradition in English. (The development of Quebec poetry is, of course, a separate story, one I am not competent to discuss, though I can admire the works of Alain Grandbois, St.-Denys-Garneau, Anne Hébert, Gaston Miron and others.)

When I first began to teach Canadian literature in 1965, and to read widely within it, I was moved to write a brief (and very partial) history as one section of a longish poem called "Macdonald Park." Macdonald's park is, of course, Canada and the Canada that is to be. Reading the earlier and later writers I was fascinated by what seemed to be going on in their work and felt that I myself was a participant in the ongoing process of discovery and creation of self and country. It is in that spirit—as poet and critic and teacher and Canadian—that I write now. I cannot pretend to a very great intellectual or emotional detachment.

I am aware, of course of a general debt to such acutely intelligent critics as George Woodcock, Malcolm Ross, Northrop Frye, Margaret Atwood, and D.G. Jones. But I feel as well that I have my own slant on things, a perspective different from theirs, my own idea of what is "Canadian." After a number of years of reading and teaching I have wanted to put this on record, since I believe that there is still much room in this field for a variety of approaches and insights.

It is dangerous, as we all know, to announce that this or that characteristic or tendency is *peculiarly* Canadian (though our popular journalists never stop doing it). And it may be that nothing is exclusively Canadian, that what happens repeatedly in Canada happens as well elsewhere for similar reasons. But I think our literature does demonstrate certain characteristics in certain patterns or conformations, and these latter may surely be said to be Canadian. The obsession with space, with enclosure and openness, that persists in our poetry is surely Canadian in the forms that it takes, even if it may exist as well in other literatures.

Again, the complexities and anomalies of the Canadian situation where a relatively small population is concentrated in disparate regions with an

immense territory are such that there exists in our most serious and characteristic creative literature a particular kind of irony that is not always very
well understood elsewhere. A pervasive ambivalence characterizes the poem
that is Canada. Herein lies our actual and potential strength (and our
survival) as well as our past and present weakness. Beyond the undoubted
obsession with survival are other overlapping concerns, or depths within
depths: the complex search for harmony in continuing diversity, for
communion and community among people and between land and people;
and, related to this, our northern mysticism, a longing for unity with the
world that leads to a greater and greater openness to and acceptance of the
beautiful and terrifying universe in flux. This is the ultimately religious
concern that informs the Canadian poetic idiom developed by writers like
Al Purdy and Margaret Avison. I want, in the linked series of essays that
follows, to discuss the evolving styles and structures of such poetry.

I believe that a work of art attempts to capture the universe (to
"swallow" life, as Northrop Frye—in *The Educated Imagination*—has it),
to be a microcosm or model. What the work of art conveys then is its own
structure, its own design, which is an attempt to capture the design or larger
rhythm of the universe as it "unfolds" in human consciousness. This is the
meaning of artistic form now and in the past. In this sense, all art is
religious. I know that many creative writers may disagree with me, but my
belief is that whether or not they know it they are performing a religious
function—the function of the shaman who attempts to control the weather
—except that in the context of our modern technological society and of
Western man's intellectual history, it is wider understanding and greater
emotional balance for author and reader alike that are the aims rather than
more external forms of power.

This work is not, strictly speaking, a history of Canadian poetry. It is too
selective, since only work of a certain quality, that is, formal self-
realization, very fully reveals that poem-that-is-Canada that interests me,
and I have little inclination to dwell on the earnest bumblings and
occasional successes of most of the nineteenth-century poets, which may
well be a useful task for social and literary historians. I have proceeded
chronologically, because I believe that the development of certain Canadian
formal and thematic continuities can best be observed in this way. But there
is also reference backwards and forwards, since I perceive Canadian poetry
as one evolving organism.

I write as a practising poet who can make, one hopes, intelligent
comments on the work of other poets. The kind of critic I admire most is
the man or woman who is engaged with the world and at the same time with
the work of artists who are engaged with the world. Among Canadian
critics one might single out George Woodcock, who seems, in his critical

books and in his biographies as well as in his many books on other than
strictly literary subjects, to be a man engaged with the world and making
sense of the world. The intellectual scheme, the search for an ultimate
structure in Western literature at large, of a critical theorist such as
Northrop Frye is impressive and is certainly intellectually stimulating,
providing as it does a framework for Frye's brilliant insights of a more
particular nature, but I think the artist is always aware that life is much
more complex and open-ended—that anything that he says about it may
well prove eventually to be, at best, an approximation of its totality, its
marvellous variety, of the way in which it is always changing itself. The
artist attempts to capture that flux, suspecting that his best work is still an
approximation. I think the critic ought to feel that way too.

One convenient way of examining the development of Canadian poetry is
to see it in terms of four stages. First there are the pioneers—those British
North American Victorians whose task was somehow to adapt the forms
and modes of their British and classical literary education to the experience
and overwhelming physical reality of the new land. D.C. Scott is the
Confederation poet who is able, in ways that I shall discuss, to carry this
adaptation furthest both technically and symbolically; and it has long been
evident to most observers that E.J. Pratt is the man who was best able to
utilize the large gestures and narrative forms of the great Elizabethan and
Romantic poets of the parent tradition in order to transform Canadian
history and geography into national myth. This had its drawbacks and
clumsinesses, however, imposing as it did past European metrical and linear
norms on the discontinous spaces of the wild future land to which their
applicability was real but necessarily limited. Nevertheless, it seems the
inevitable expression of a society moving very rapidly from heroic
pioneering to sophisticated technology even as it moved psychically from
Europe to America. Scott and Pratt, and before them, Lampman with his
"City of the End of Things," are transitional poets. In the second stage the
modernists of a younger generation that is now elderly offered as an alternative to the force and narrative drive of Pratt a new compression of
thought and meaning, a metaphysical subtlety and sophistication, and a
formal eclecticism that were inspired by the theory and practice of T.S.
Eliot, Ezra Pound, and other poets (mostly American) of the 1920's. And
though this movement, which rejected vociferously the lingering influence
of the Confederation school, might be seen, at least in its weakest and most
derivative products, to represent a somewhat updated colonialism, this does
not characterize adequately its best results, the finer poems of F.R. Scott,
A.J.M. Smith, Ralph Gustafson, John Glassco, Dorothy Livesay and
others, which made possible the distinctive work of such "modernist"
Canadian masters as A.M. Klein, P.K. Page, Earle Birney and Irving

Layton, who are able in their best and most mature work to combine the vitality and vigour of Pratt with the technical sophistication and metaphysical wit of Smith.

But eclecticism and versatility carry one only so far. There was still another stage of adaptation that would go beyond versatility to a further mastery: the assumption by the inheritors and assimilators of the first two stages of a distinctive Canadian free-verse idiom that is more nearly, instead of just approximately, appropriate to the new reality of stretching space and multiple perspective. This occurs most impressively in the poems of Al Purdy and Margaret Avison, though one may find it at times as well in the work of older and younger poets such as R.G. Everson, Louis Dudek, Raymond Souster, D.G. Jones, Phyllis Webb, and others. Here technique is what Dennis Lee once termed a "clean fit...which seems to be skin, not costume," that is, here one is less aware of technique or form as such than one is when reading the highly wrought and variously beautiful or effective works of our Canadian modernists. For Purdy and Avison poetry is process (as is life anywhere, though this insists upon itself much more in a vast, open land); process of language and consciousness and finished work are one thing. And this is a lesson that has been learned by the most notable poets of the generation after Purdy, for example, Margaret Atwood, Gwendolyn MacEwen, Michael Ondaatje, John Newlove, Dennis Lee himself, who constitute a fourth stage, the explosion of innumerable new talents in the heady 1960's. I find it significant that some of the most notable of these poets of my own generation, who are now in mid-career, creeping into middle age, have wanted to express their vision of life and of changing Canada in works of prose-fiction as well, so I have concentrated on this phenomenon since it is impossible to do anything like justice to *all* of the interesting poets who are writing and publishing now. The poet-novelists are seeking to extend themselves, to re-discover the largeness and scope of Pratt, who remains a somewhat ambiguous monument in their ancestral past, in new ways more appropriate to their own time. Leonard Cohen is perhaps the most notable new pioneer of this new departure.

My central concern has been the poem that is Canada and Canadians. A poet beginning today may assimilate all the past stages by which poetry has assimilated or "swallowed" life in Canada. ("Let me swallow it whole and be strong," writes John Newlove in "Resources, Certain Earths.") The Canadian land and the Canadian community as it is and as it might be; this is the distinctive context for a poetry concerned with the universal matter of life, love and death on the earth. The journey of the Canadian poet—with the important milestones and particular characteristics that are my concern in what follows—has been and is a continuing journey toward wholeness of comprehension and of being.

PART ONE

Half-Breeds: The Pioneers

Dear Bad Poets

Tentative Approaches to the Canadian Space

James Reaney has written in passing of the "dear bad poets/who wrote/ Early in Canada/And never were of note" ("To the Avon River above Stratford, Canada"). These were the Ur-poets, these McLachlans, Camerons, Drummonds, Johnsons, and others, the necessary, competent drudges who prepared the way for the more accomplished, more genuinely native poets who followed. If they are of note, it is less for the quality of their work than for their brave pioneering and their exemplification of the colonial poet's problems. Their failures and moderate successes were instructive to their successors. There were, pre-eminently, the three Charleses: Heavysege, Sangster, and Mair. There were Thomas Chandler Haliburton's associates Joseph Howe and Oliver Goldsmith. One might even, for fun, throw in the four Jameses—Gay, McIntyre, Gillis, and MacRae—whose efforts have earned them honourable place among the world's "great bad poets." McIntyre, who penned the immortal "Ode on the Mammoth Cheese," is surely the Canadian McGonagall:

> We have seen thee, queen of cheese
> Lying quietly at your ease,
> Gently fanned by evening breeze,
> Thy fair form no flies dare seize.
>
> All gaily dressed soon you'll go
> To the great Provincial show
> To be admired by many a beau
> In the city of Toronto
>
> .   .   .   .
>
> We'rt thou suspended from balloon,
> You'd cast a shade even at noon,

> Folks would think it was the moon
> About to fall and crush them soon.

This is certainly Canadian content and much funnier than the more recent, pleasingly bad poems in Paul Hiebert's *Sarah Binks*. Perhaps the combination of "thee" and "your," "thou" and "you'd" even represents a genuinely Canadian compromise between archaic and colloquial diction.

Sangster, whom the nineteenth-century versifier Susanna Moodie dubbed "the Canadian Wordsworth," wrote of the thousand islands and the Saguenay in Spenserian stanzas employing diction that echoes Wordsworth and Keats at once:

> Over the darkening waters! on through scenes
> Whose unimaginable wildness fills
> The mind with joy insensate, and weans
> The soul from earth, to Him whose Presence thrills
> All Beauty as all Truth.

> "The St. Lawrence and the Saguenay"

Goldsmith wrote of a rising Canadian village in the manner of his great-uncle's "Deserted Village." Charles Heavysege wrote pseudo-Shakespearean closet-dramas on biblical subjects, making no direct or obvious references to Canada. Like the young A.M. Klein later on, he found it more congenial to express himself in terms of the "timeless" old-world culture. In a long life involving Ontario imperialism, horsewhipping, the first Riel rebellion, and theatrical drama, Charles Mair occasionally described minute Canadian particulars with some of the sharp focus later found in Roberts and Lampman:

> Now one may mark the spider trim his web
> From bough to bough, and sorrow at the fate
> Of many a sapless fly quite picked and bare,
> Still hanging lifeless in the silken mesh,
> Or muse upon the maze of insect brede
> Which finds a home and feeds upon the leaves
> Till naught but fibre-skeletons are hung
> From branch to branch up to the highest twig.

> "August"

Most of these examples suggest some incongruity between Canadian subject-matter and the English Romantic-Victorian poetic idiom. But why should these poets write in a fashion different from their British contemporaries? They *were* Victorians and certainly felt themselves to be as British as any other of Her Majesty's subjects. They had no notions of attending to an "American language."

Why then did they fail to write good British poetry about Canada? Is it simply that they were mediocre poets? In a way, yes. They could only work with the literary education and models that they had, and they failed to see that these were not always particularly appropriate to the Canadian reality that they were attempting to articulate. John Matthews, whose ideas about these poets and their cultural dilemma are very helpful, has observed that the successes of the later Confederation poets have much to do with their ability to apply the Romantic-Victorian idiom selectively to the Canadian environment. Matthews' account of Lampman's "Morning on the Lièvre" in *Tradition in Exile* shows this selective adaptation at work.

It is Wordworth's power of precise description rather than his passages of lofty sentiment that prove most useful to Roberts and Lampman. The lofty sentiments belonged to a tamer, more settled, more manageable country. The eeriness of Canadian space, the apparent emptiness, the silence required another expression, one the Canadian poets could not yet utter. Meanwhile, what they could do was to describe the particular things that inhabited the vastness in such a way that the space around these things could be felt too. There were perhaps largely unconscious native tendencies towards imagism and, in Duncan Campbell Scott, towards free verse as well. In this way it became possible, and necessary, to move formally towards a North American language, one that would be, in Al Purdy's hands, for example, significantly different from the kindred "American language" fathered by Walt Whitman. Canadian poetry had to find its own way out of the English confinement of those hedge-rows, rhyme and metre.

Sangster felt the emptiness but did not sharply delineate the particulars in a way that might reveal the strange spaces around each particular thing. Mair sometimes looked hard at particulars, as the above quotation shows, forgetting about the vast context. Charles G.D. Roberts provided in his best poems, such as "The Tantramar Revisited," a kind of synthesis, one that Lampman and D.C. Scott, in poems in which individual things are perceived as separate and distinct but also as parts of the vast cosmos, developed further. There is then further development of description, cosmic consciousness and narrative from Scott to Pratt, Pratt to Birney, Birney to Purdy, and Purdy to younger poets. This is one stream that leads us to contemporary Canadian poetry, though not the only one.

There was also the possibility of presenting the external environment as it lives in the mind, in the dream-life of the poet. This is a way of at least temporarily minimizing the strangeness, of psychologically containing the danger and the void, that one finds in certain passages and poems by Isabella Valancy Crawford and very notably in Bliss Carman's "Low Tide on Grand Pré." The exuberant metaphors and surrealistic visions of A.M. Klein, Irving Layton, Leonard Cohen, Gwendolyn MacEwen, and others constitute a more recent attempt at the containment or "swallowing" of the world in order to feel at one with it. In a sense, all poets do this in the very act of composing a poem, making of it a microcosm or self-contained world within the world; but there is a difference in emphasis between the realist poet who attempts objective description and that poet who presents the external world as fully symbolic of his own psychic state. One becomes aware in any truly successful poem of the ultimate continuity of inner and outer worlds in human consciousness, but the perspective or point of departure is different in each case.

Isabella Crawford, who died at the age of thirty-seven in 1887, felt her way towards Indian myth and animistic consciousness as an expression of the spirit of the place and knew the power of metaphor. Here are two of the most quoted passages:

> The late, last thunders of the summer crash'd
> Where shriek'd great eagles, lords of naked cliffs.
> The pulseless forest, lock'd and interlock'd
> So closely, bough with bough, and leaf with leaf,
> So serf'd by its own wealth, that while from high
> The moons of summer kiss'd its green-gloss'd locks,
> And round its knees the merry West Wind danc'd;
> And round its ring, compacted emerald,
> The South Wind crept on moccasins of flame...
>
>   .   .   , ...
>
> And Max car'd little for the blotted sun,
> And nothing for the startl'd, outshone stars;
> For Love, once set within a lover's breast,
> Has its own Sun, its own peculiar sky,
> All one great daffodil, on which do lie
> The sun, the moon, the stars, all seen at once
> And never setting, but all shining straight
> Into the faces of the trinity—
> The one belov'd, the lover, and sweet Love.

                                        "Malcolm's Katie"

The first passage brings to life, as in an Emily Carr painting with its flow and rhythm, the primitive vision of an animistic world; the second, with its trinity and heavenly flower, reminds us that Crawford read Dante. Again one is conscious of the juxtaposition of America and Europe. In youth Crawford lived near the bush, but she nevertheless acquired the high literary culture of the European past, a situation repeated in the life of Margaret Atwood a century later.

In a few passages and poems Crawford is much more than the "dear bad" poetess who penned unwieldy and melodramatic narratives of life in the bush. One of her best shorter poems is "The Dark Stag":

> A startled stag, the blue-grey Night,
>   Leaps down beyond black pines.
> Behind—a length of yellow light—
>   The hunter's arrow shines:
> His moccasins are stained with red,
>   He bends upon his knee,
> From covering peaks his shafts are sped....
>
>   .   .   .   .
>
> His feet are in the waves of space;
>   His antlers broad and dun
> He lowers; he turns his velvet face
>   To front the hunter, Sun....
>
>   .   .   .   .
>
> Shaft after shaft the red Sun speeds:
>   Rent the stag's dappled side,
> His breast, fanged by the shrill winds, bleeds,
>   He staggers on the tide;
> He feels the hungry waves of space
>   Rush at him high and blue....
>
>   .   .   .   .
>
> His branches smite the wave—with cries
>   The loud winds pause and flag
> He sinks in space—red glow the skies,
> The brown earth crimsons as he dies,
>   The strong and dusky stag.

The extended conceits make the coming of dawn a dramatic, living process. The terror of "the waves of space" and the predatory nature of this world are expressed in forceful, primitive terms. Description of the Canadian wild may be very generalized, but the mythic figures of stag and hunters are sharply limned. Appropriately, they contain the wild as the poet's imagination contains them. One may even sense, though there is no reference in the poem to either, nor to any story about them, the faint ghosts of Actaeon, the mighty hunter who was turned into a stag and killed by his own hounds, and of Apollo the sun-god, behind the stag and the Indian hunter-sun. Crawford probably did not have these figures consciously in mind, but they existed in the collective imagination of the culture and could therefore reinforce, in a subliminal way, the impact of the parallel Indian figure of the predatory universe. Certainly, the "Greek" quality of elemental Canada—not pastoral but the terrifying force conveyed by the myths of a cruel ancient land—appears to have impressed itself on Roberts and Carman in the nineteenth century and on Hugh MacLennan, Irving Layton, and Leonard Cohen, who dreams of an Indian "red acropolis" in *Beautiful Losers*, in the mid-twentieth century. This kind of imaginative leap to the archetypal figure that conveys the dimensions and essential character of a world is what distinguishes Crawford's best work from that of her more pedestrian contemporaries. Here, as in Roberts and Carman, the true poetry of the Canadian space begins.

Mountaineers and Swimmers

Roberts and Carman Revisited

> Roberts, moving yet on the high
> green hill over Tantramar, needed
> the distance from which he looks.
> Carman, his cousin, not so lucky
> as to have found distance,
> made of our vagueness
> a virtue, a voice for loss
> and the uncertain floods of longing.[1]

It is interesting to compare Roberts's poem "The Tantramar Revisited" with Bliss Carman's "Low Tide on Grand Pré." Both poems are concerned (as is Wordsworth's "Tintern Abbey," their likely ancestor) with loss and the return to a remembered landscape. But Roberts remains aloof from the beloved landscape, attempting to hold it unchanged in his mind:

> Only in these green hills, aslant to the sea, no change!
> Here where the road that has climbed from the inland
>   valleys and woodlands,
> Dips from the hill-tops down, straight to the base of the
>   hills—
> Here, from my vantage-ground, I can see the scattering
>   houses,
> Stained with time, set warm in orchards, meadows and
>   wheat,
> Dotting the broad bright slopes outspread to southward
>   and eastward,
> Wind-swept all day long, blown by the southeast wind.

From his vantage-ground Roberts surveys his country's stretching space but also recalls the precise details of interiors:

> Ah, how well I remember those wide red flats, above
>   tide-mark
> Pale with scurf of the salt, seamed and baked in the sun!
> Well I remember the piles of blocks and ropes, and the
>   net-reels
> Wound with the beaded nets, dripping and dark from
>   the sea!
> Now at this season the nets are unwound; they hang
>   from the rafters
> Over the fresh-stowed hay in upland barns, and the
>   wind
> Blows all day through the chinks, with the streaks of
>   sunlight, and sways them
> Softly at will; or they lie heaped in the gloom of a loft.

Here is a power of observation like that of a Maritime realist painter. Roberts's verse is Homeric in its sweep and its enumeration of particulars, as Lampman was probably the first to note.[2] As the Tantramar lands are bounded and preserved by dykes, so the poet attempts to hold them in timeless suspension in the microcosm of a poem whose repetitions of phrase and whose rhythmic rise and return themselves embody the sense of an endless cycle:

> Yet, as I sit and watch, this present peace of the
>   landscape—
> Stranded boats, these reels empty and idle, the hush,
> One grey hawk slow-wheeling above yon cluster of
>   haystacks—
> More than the old-time stir this stillness welcomes me
>   home.
> Ah the old-time stir, how once it stung me with
>   rapture—
> Old-time sweetness, the winds freighted with honey and
>   salt!
> Yet will I stay my steps and not go down to the
>   marshland—
> Muse and recall far off, rather remember than see—
> Lest on too close sight I miss the darling illusion,

Spy at their task even here the hands of chance and
change.

Roberts holds the landscape of remembered happiness at a distance. He
seems to want to be godlike, above the battle. By contrast, Bliss Carman
immerses himself in the intensely re-lived experience of love and loss in
"Low Tide on Grand Pré." The landscape is made expressive both of his
remembered joy and of the grief that followed it:

> A grievous stream that to and fro
> Athrough the fields of Acadie
> Goes wandering, as if to know
> Why one beloved face should be
> So long from home and Acadie.
>
> Was it a year or lives ago
> We took the grasses in our hands,
> And caught the summer flying low
> Over the waving meadow lands,
> And held it there between our hands?
>
> The while the river at our feet—
> A drowsy inland meadow stream—
> At set of sun the after-heat
> Made running gold, and in the gleam
> We freed our birch upon the stream.
>
> .   .   .   .
>
> Then all your face grew light, and seemed
> To hold the shadow of the sun;
> The evening faltered, and I deemed
> That time was ripe, and years had done
> Their wheeling underneath the sun.
>
> So all desire and all regret,
> And fear and memory, were naught;
> One to remember or forget
> The keen delight our hands had caught;
> Morrow and yesterday were naught.
>
> The night has fallen, and the tide....
> Now and again comes drifting home,
> Across these aching barrens wide,
> A sigh like driven wind or foam:
> In grief the flood is bursting home.

At first everything is hazy, as in an impressionist painting or a romantic film resorting to slow-motion. For a magical moment it had once seemed as if love could stop time. The captured bird, the slowed stream, the rhyme-scheme, and the metre reinforce this idea. But the final stanza returns us to the present with a vengeance. The bird of happiness, or youth, escapes; it is the sun, and not "time," that falls like a ripe fruit; days and summers end; the tide comes in. The hands of chance and change are victorious here, too, but unlike Roberts, Carman makes no attempt to distance himself from the situation. He lets it, so to speak, wash over him.

Roberts, at his best in realistic poems of observation, is the man who cultivates Olympian detachment; Carman, the lyrical impressionist who advised "paint the vision, not the view," is the man who plunges into emotional experience.[3] Many of our best poets later on have been either mountaineers, who free their myths from fact (Pratt, Birney, Purdy, Newlove), or swimmers who explore their own depths (Klein, Layton, Cohen, MacEwen, Atwood). These figures actually occur in some of our most significant poems, a thing not surprising in a country with so much rock and water about. Sometimes, as in Frank Scott's poem "Lakeshore," the figures of swimmer and man on mountain, in this instance Noah, are combined. Mountains evoke objectivity and a god's-eye view of the dangerous external world, water the ever-changing depths of the self, the collective unconscious and the racial and evolutionary past. But it is a difference of emphasis or method rather than of essential purpose that I mean to stress, since all good poems embody the relationship between inner and outer worlds, and great art is subjective and objective at once. Consciousness involves a continuing interaction between fact and dream.[4]

Roberts was the first Canadian poet of impressive achievement. He deserves his special position as the father of Canadian poetry, and, as we know, he gave particular impetus and inspiration to Archibald Lampman, who in turn encouraged Duncan Campbell Scott. In this context Lampman's well-known account of his discovery of *Orion* is worth our examination:

It was like a voice from some new paradise of art calling us to be up and doing. A little after sunrise I got up and went out into the college grounds. The air, I remember, was full of the odour and cool sunshine of the spring morning. The dew was thick upon the grass. All the birds of our Maytime seemed to be singing in the oaks, and there were even a few adder-tongues and trilliums still blossoming on the slope of the little ravine. But everything was transfigured for me beyond descrip-tion, bathed in an old world radiance of beauty [by] the magic of the lines that were sounding in my ears, those divine verses, as they seemed to me, with their Tennyson-like richness and strange, earth-loving, Greekish flavour.[5]

What is interesting in this passage, apart from the attractive enthusiasm of youth, is the suggestion that poetry, acting upon the mind and senses, fuses two worlds, the immediate physical beauty of Canadian spring ("our Maytime") and the old world, which is, to the Canadian on the outskirts of civilization, a dream-world of the cultural past. These poets, as British North Americans, felt the need to impose this European cultural past on Canada.

Possibly, the savagery and mystery of Greek myth—the stories of Orion, Marsyas, and Actaeon for Roberts—prove more appropriate to the savage and beautiful character of the new land than the high art of settled Europe. A classical education could take on a new meaning in a harsh but lovely land.[6] Looking at Roberts's poems one feels that something in the nature of the new land could, with some degree of appropriateness, be rendered in terms of a "Greekish" and "earth-loving" (though hardly a Tennysonian) sensibility. These lines from "Orion" are an example:

> all the limitless blue sea
> Brightening with laughter many a league around
> Wind-wrinkled, keel-uncloven, far below;
> And far above the bright sky-neighbouring peaks;
> And all around the broken precipices,
> Cleft-rooted pines swung over falling foam,
> And silver vapours flushed with the wide flood
> Of crimson slanted from the opening east.

This could as easily be Canada as Greece; the passage has the same sense of distances as does "The Tantramar Revisited" but not, unfortunately, the complementary vivid focus on particulars. Instead there is this "classical" description of a woman:

> For there beside him, veilèd in a mist
> Where—through the enfolded splendour issued forth—
> As delicate music unto one asleep
> Through mist of dreams flows softly—all her hair
> A mist of gold flung down about her feet,
> Her dewy, cool, pink fingers parting it
> Till glowing lips, and half-seen snowy curves
> Like Parian stone, unnerved him, waited SHE.

This mélange of mist, music, gold and marble tangled up in a somewhat labyrinthine syntax may have excited the undergraduate Lampman, but it is now more likely to suggest a coy, artfully posed statue to us than the warmblooded woman called for in Roberts's version of the story of Orion. The "Tennysonian" sensibility prevails.

Roberts is at his best in almost purely descriptive landscape poems. He shies away from any very acute consideration of human relationships, and his overtly philosophical poems are too grandly general to be very convincing. Aside from "The Tantramar Revisited," it is the sonnets—"The Potato Harvest," "The Pea-Fields," and "The Winter Fields" in particular—that constitute his lasting achievement as a poet. Except for the delightful "Pea-Fields," these poems tend to be sombre in tone.

I like to ask students whether these poems make them think of another well-known poet, and someone usually volunteers the name of Robert Frost. "The Winter Fields" is similar in theme to Frost's poems "The Onset" and "Desert Places." In all three of these poems there is sharp observation of the coming of winter, but there is this important difference: Frost is strongly present in his poems both as distinctive voice and as character; Roberts is the remote, god-like observer. Unlike his pupil, Lampman, he would never offer such self-revelation as is found in this famous passage from Frost's "Desert Places":

> They cannot scare me with their empty spaces
> Between stars—on stars where no human race is.
> I have it in me so much nearer home
> To scare myself with my own desert places.

It is also interesting that Frost, an American wrestling with the optimistic ghost of Roberts's and Carman's kinsman, Emerson, is able to suggest the possibility imaged in the snow's blankness, that existence may be a meaningless void, while the Canadian Roberts refuses, in his official, philosophical poems, the possible implications of the description of New Brunswick's "amber wastes of sky," "wide flats," "lonely flush," "lonely reaches," "wastes of hard and meagre weeds," "brackish pools and ditches blind," "low-lying pastures of the wind," "crying knives," and "sleet and frost that bites like steel" in his own descriptive sonnets, affirming instead (in the windily unconvincing "In the Wide Awe and Wisdom of the Night") an Emersonian "august infinitude of Man." It is not so far, after all, from New Hampshire to New Brunswick. In his anguished doubt and self-doubt the somewhat younger Frost became a modern poet. Roberts maintained an official Victorian optimism, but only, it appears, by refusing to enter completely his native space. Still, the best poems remain to show us that he began the journey.

Carman too exhibits a certain cultural schizophrenia. The official optimism of British and American taste-makers sorts ill with his sense of the haunted quality of his homeland. His emotions are usually expressed in terms of natural processes, most notably those of autumn's colourful decline and decay. Characteristic images with which he seems to identify himself are tiny flowers, moths, children, or waifs, whose beauty is ephemeral and doomed. He feels the eeriness of the Canadian space:

> Come, for the night is cold
> The ghostly moonlight fills
> Hollow and rift and fold
> Of the eerie Ardise hills!

> The windows of my room
> Are dark with bitter frost,
> The stillness aches with doom
> Of something loved and lost.

In this poem, "A Northern Vigil," the absence of an imaginary girl named Guendolyn, who is characterized as the soul of the place, is lamented; without her this place is empty of spirit or meaning. The early Carman seems quite happy with Edgar Allan Poe's myth of the lost beloved, and perhaps he feels himself, as Poe apparently did, to be a culturally displaced person.

A little later, having gone completely American, he writes his cheerful but empty vagabondia poems to protest, unconvincingly, a Whitmanesque optimism. There are also, however, poems on classical themes like "The Dead Faun," which objectifies Carman's own sense of death and loss in terms of the classical world, the successful adaptations of Sappho, and a mixing of mythologies that foreshadows the work of Leonard Cohen. In a number of ways Carman was the Leonard Cohen of his time, a restless man with a remarkable lyric gift much appreciated by an international public; one could even view Cohen's song "Suzanne" as an updated version of Carman's "Lady of the Rain": in each a versatile mother-goddess or Isis-figure is celebrated.[7]

Carman's best poems convey a sense of loss, of that psychological and cultural displacement that many sensitive Canadians have experienced. He does not, like Crawford and Lampman and Scott, go forward from this to engage the gods of place on their own ground. But he leaves, in his own vague, musical and impressionistic fashion, an atmosphere, a sense of the problem.

Notes

1. Tom Marshall, "Macdonald Park," *The Silences of Fire* (Toronto: Macmillan, 1969).
2. A.J.M. Smith, ed., *Masks of Poetry* (Toronto: McClelland and Stewart, 1962).
3. Carl F. Klinck, et al., *Literary History of Canada* (Toronto: University of Toronto Press, 1965), p. 413.
4. "I often wish," said Carman, "that I could rid the world of the tyranny of facts. What are facts but compromises? A fact merely marks the point where we have agreed to let investigation cease. Investigate further and your fact disappears. Under the scrutiny of thought all facts are alike. from the atom to the universe...and they dissolve" (James Cappon, "Bliss Carman's Beginnings," *Queen's Quarterly* 36 [Autumn 1929]: 657). More recently, William Irwin Thompson writes interestingly of the physicists Weizsäcker and Heisenberg and their awareness of the "psychological implications of the quantum theory" in his *Passages About Earth* (New York: Harper and Row, 1974): "if the modes of perceiving [subatomic particles] through laboratory instruments and mathematics alter the material itself, then, as Heisenberg would say, we no longer have a science of nature, but a science of the mind's knowledge about nature" (p. 91). Similarly, the most basic techniques of poetry (which are extensions of the body's modes of sense-perception) alter the object of the poet's attention, however objective he may think he is being. His true "subject," and what it is that demands that he find the exact form for his utterance, is himself experiencing the world.
5. "Two Canadian Poets: A Lecture, 1891," *Masks of Poetry*, p. 30.
6. Similarly, a biblical story could express man's relationship to a cruel nature. Northrop Frye has elucidated the hidden "Canadian content" of Heavysege's "Jephthah's Daughter" (*The Bush Garden*, [Toronto: Anansi, 1971], pp. 150-51).
7. In a letter to Michael Ondaatje in 1967 or so I called Cohen (rather unfairly) "the Bliss Carman of the sixties." Later, looking at *Read Canadian*, I noticed that Dennis Lee had had at some point a similar thought.

Archibald Lampman

More Facts and Dreams

In his celebrated poem "Heat" Lampman does what Roberts will not do: he places himself in the centre of his picture. His eye moves from far to near things, pointing up in a dialectical fashion, as Desmond Pacey in *Ten Canadian Poets* has demonstrated, all sorts of contrasts and pairs of opposites. Unlike Bliss Carman, he does not, in this poem, present the landscape as a symbolic representation of his own inner goings-on, nor does he view it in mythopoeic terms, like Isabella Crawford; he defines himself as separate in his encounter with the environment, concluding

> In the full furnace of this hour
> My thoughts grow keen and clear.

The land's summer heat becomes a crucible in which his individual thoughts, perhaps even his "clearer self," may be shaped. Thus he detaches himself intellectually, engaging the environment but refusing to be immersed in it. He asserts human will and values in the face of the natural world.

There is another, contrasted furnace in Lampman's work, one that has a less happy relation to human individuality—the infernal furnace of his "City of the End of Things":

> A flaming terrible and bright
> Shakes all the stalking shadows there,
> Across the walls, across the floors,
> And shifts upon the upper air
> From out a thousand furnace doors;
> And all the while an awful sound
> Keeps roaring on continually,

And crashes in the ceaseless round
Of a gigantic harmony.
Through its grim depths re-echoing
And all its weary height of walls,
With measured roar and iron ring,
The inhuman music lifts and falls.
Where no thing rests and no man is,
And only fire and night hold sway;
The heat, the thunder and the hiss
Cease not, and change not, night nor day.
And moving at unheard commands,
The abysses and vast fires between,
Flit figures that with clanking hands
Obey a hideous routine.

Was this partly inspired by a particularly hot and noisy nineteenth-century summer in Ottawa? The question is not wholly facetious or simple-minded. Here is a vivid picture of mechanical hell in an honourable Victorian tradition that goes back at least as far as Blake and his reaction to the Industrial Revolution. Lampman's extraordinary sensitivity to sound, evident in his best poetry of nature, becomes here a horror of mechanical noise. Noises obviously upset him, even in nineteenth-century Ottawa, as his sonnet "The Railway Station," with its picture of lives controlled by a moving machine, indicates. This oversensitivity was an advantage in presenting his vision, not to be found in any other Canadian poet of the time, of a mechanized hell in which human beings are robbed of their souls. Later, the theme of machine-as-environment is continued in Grove's *Master of the Mill* and E.J. Pratt's *Titanic*, not to mention the social poems of Dorothy Livesay and others. All of these writers are concerned with the swiftness of Canada's passage from a pioneer society to a highly sophisticated technological society, and also with the continuing juxtaposition of the primitive and the mechanical.

Lampman's description of his infernal city is more effective than the allegory that follows in the latter part of the poem. The latter part of the poem describes three masters of power and a soulless idiot who cannot die. Possibly the three are the industrial powers dominating Canada and the idiot Canada itself, "that great retarded giant to the north" as an American satirical magazine, the *National Lampoon*, once had it, but the nineteenth-century idiom is too generalized to be certain. Still, the image of the idiot, sitting at the gateway of the modern industrialized world "looking toward the lightless north/beyond the reach of memories," which signifies perhaps both the sheer mindless corporeal bulk of the land and the Canadian people themselves totally bereft of the last shred of vision or imagination—not so much a sleeping as a drugged giant—is a compelling one. The image is akin to Thomas Chandler Haliburton's vision of New Brunswick as a sleeping monster in *The Clockmaker*.

Lampman apparently felt that man could define and realize himself in his encounter with nature, but that the machine might well rob him of his human and unique values. In nature he feels his autonomy as a thinking being; the mechanical appears to threaten his sanity.

But nature has its terrors too, as well as the beauty, peace and regenerative effect suggested in "April," "The Frogs," and the highly successful "Among the Timothy," and Lampman is increasingly aware of them. Like Robert Frost a little later, and unlike Charles G.D. Roberts, he begins to perceive the possibility of void.

> a region where no faintest gust
> Of life comes ever, but the power of night,
> Dwells stupendous and sublime,
> Limitless and void and lonely.
>
> "Alcyone"

"The Autumn Waste" and "Winter Evening" convey a similar feeling:

> soon from height to height,
> With silence and the sharp unpitying stars,
> Stern creeping frosts, and winds that touch like steel,
> Out of the depth beyond the eastern bars,
> Glittering and still shall come the awful night.
>
> "Winter Evening"

Against this death Lampman poses what he calls, in a number of poems, the "dream" or "vision":

> Fast drives the snow, and no man comes this way;
> The hills grow wintry white, and bleak winds moan
> About the naked uplands. I alone
> Am neither sad, nor shelterless, nor grey,
> Wrapped round with thought, content to watch and dream.
>
> "In November"

To "dream" seems to be, in a number of poems, the human ability to become detached from the cold, or hot, world, and dwell in a mental, visionary world that Lampman can suggest but not articulate very clearly. One can only guess that when he watches the snow and "dreams" he is affirming the autonomy and creativity of the human mind, the power of "jail-break/and re-creation" that Margaret Avison demonstrates in her sonnet "Snow." Lampman, a sonneteer of considerable skill, nevertheless lacks Avison's great breadth of technical and imaginative resources. There are limits to an idiom that insists on austere, imagistic clarity; Avison's profusion of metaphors, as rich and rather more controlled than Isabella Crawford's, can better demonstrate the symbol-making powers of the untrammelled mind and senses and reveal as well the active consciousness as interface between inner and outer worlds. Lampman can only approach this.

Moreover, the visionary power, this uniquely human faculty, tends to desert him:

> And those high moods of mine that sometime made
> My heart a heaven, opening like a flower
> A sweeter world where I in wonder strayed,
> Begirt with shapes of beauty and the power
> Of dreams that moved through that enchanted clime
> With changing breaths of rhyme,
> Were all gone lifeless now.
>
> "Among the Timothy"

Whither is fled the visionary gleam? In this poem Lampman regains it as the calm of the natural setting helps to ease his mind into the alpha-waves of revery. (Must the "gleam" be inexorably lost, as Wordsworth lost it? Perhaps it need never be lost, if the poet has access to religious and sensory disciplines such as yoga, meditation, or Yeats's exercises in conjuring up symbols from the collective unconscious. These were not, as far as I know, available to Wordsworth, but even to the poet-sons of protestant parsons in late nineteenth-century Canada they might have been in time.)

Often enough, Lampman's vision tends to give way to a sense of void:

> Down in the west
> The brimming plains beneath the sunset rest,
> One burning sea of gold. Soon, soon shall fly
> The glorious vision, and the hours shall feel
> A mightier master; soon from height to height,
> With silence and the sharp unpitying stars

and so on into one of the more sinister passages already quoted. Is the
visionary world then purely mental, a quirk of human sense-perception,
brainwaves and fancy, a beautiful illusion? Or is it man's small portion of the
divine that somehow contains the outer world's violence and waste within a
larger pattern, as Lampman, and D.C. Scott after him, would like to
believe? Is the universe, in fact, as mechanical in its process as the future
city he fears, or is it informed by some divine meaning and purpose?

These questions seem to be posed though certainly not answered in
"Uplifting," in which what appears to be a domestic dispute drives the poet
to cosmic consciousness:

> We passed heart-weary from the troubled house,
> Where much of care and much of strife had been,
> A jar of tongues upon a petty scene;
> And now as from a long and tortured drouse,
> The dark returned us to our purer vows:
> The open darkness, like a friendly palm,
> And the great night was round us with her calm:
> We felt the large free wind upon our brows,
> And suddenly above us saw revealed
> The holy round of heaven—all its rime
> Of suns and planets and its nebulous rust—
> Sable and glittering like a mythic shield,
> Sown with the gold of giants and of time,
> The worlds and all their systems but as dust.

Here we have Lampman's main themes in a nutshell: the passage from a
"troubled house" (as from the city) into the open space; the calming effect
of the nonhuman world's essential neutrality, its indifference to man's
problems (as in "The Frogs"); the visionary faculty which sees the stars as a
"mythic shield" (there is another such mythic conceit in "The Sun Cup,"
but these effects, a little reminiscent of Crawford's, are rare); the "holy
round" of existence, perhaps divine, that dominates most of Lampman's
best poems; and the possibility, here only hinted, that the cycle may, after
all, be meaningless and empty, "worlds and all their systems but as dust,"
as in "The City of the End of Things" with its "hideous routine" and
"ceaseless round."

Lampman does not solve the problems he raises; a duality reigns. Life is
heaven or it is hell, depending upon one's perspective. But he appears to
move toward something like an existentialist position in his suggestion that
man must oppose his own values to the mindless and perhaps meaningless
violence of nature. In "At the Long Sault: May 1660" he indicates that the

present peace of the landscape is dependent upon the heroic resistance of men like Daulac to the savage, a theme amplified by Pratt in "Brébeuf and His Brethren." Unfortunately, both Lampman and Pratt present the Indians as personifications of the savagery of the wild without, apparently, considering that they had had to learn to survive in the wild and were resisting a stronger, encroaching culture. D.C. Scott is more aware of the tragic complexity of the situation.

Lampman opened up territory that Scott, Pratt and Birney were to explore further. He added to Roberts's power of observation the ability to think about his own, and man's, relationship to the new world and also to the industrial culture being imposed upon it. If both his social and his more personal vision remain somewhat vague because he did not, before his early death, escape what I have called the Romantic-Victorian poetic idiom, he nevertheless left poems that go right to the edge of something new and that articulate honestly and well, within the limitations of that idiom, his own inability to go further.

Half-Breeds

Duncan Campbell Scott

It has often been remarked that an important theme of colonial Canadian poetry is alienation: the alienation of races and cultures from one another, of old world from new, of culture from nature, and, either partly or wholly as a consequence of these, of man from his larger, or grander, self. Duncan Campbell Scott was able to enlarge in a highly significant way upon his friend Archibald Lampman's acute but only sketchily articulated insights into these matters. Least appreciated of the Confederation poets in his lifetime, Scott is, nevertheless, the best and most important of them, since he goes further technically, emotionally, and intellectually towards an idiom that can embody the Canadian situation. He has a much wider range than any of his colleagues and an ability to express his ideas dramatically in terms of human narrative that anticipates the method of Pratt.

The dialectical character of Scott's vision can be seen in "The Piper of Arll," his symbolic fable of the artist in exile. His piper is also a shepherd, a guardian perhaps (like Milton's Lycidas, or King David, or Jesus, for that matter) of the moral and imaginative life. Like the Canadian poet, he confronts both the beauty and the terror of a world in which violence and love co-exist:

> There were three pines above the comb
> That, when the sun flared and went down,
> Grew like three warriors reaving home
> The plunder of a burning town.
>
>   .   .   .   .
>
> And there a ship one evening stood,
> Where ship had never stood before;
> A pennon bickered red as blood
> An angel glimmered at the prore.

The bay has trees that resemble warriors and that may also suggest, in a subliminal way, crosses; the ship announces both blood and angels.

The mysterious ship also makes music, to which the piper responds appropriately;

> The piper heard an outland tongue,
> With music in the cadenced fall;
> And when the fairy lights were hung,
> The sailors gathered one and all,
>
> And leaning on the gunwales dark,
> Crusted with shells and dashed with foam,
> With all the dreaming hills to hark,
> They sang their longing songs of home.
>
> When the sweet airs had fled away,
> The piper, with a gentle breath,
> Moulded a tranquil melody
> Of lonely love and longed-for death.

The piper's song of alienation and loneliness is akin to the sailors' song of homesickness. This could be seen as a dialogue between the lonely poet in exile and the somewhat ghostly representatives of his ancestral tradition. Certainly the sailors are the piper's longed-for audience, and perhaps they are his colleagues in the art of song. At first, however, they fail to acknowledge him. In the morning he finds that the ship has fled, and, distraught, he breaks his pipe. He is cut off from the fellowship of his peers.

Like the early Canadian poets, however, he must persist in exile in order to regain his lost heritage. He mends his pipe:

> A melody began to drip
> That mingled with a ghostly thrill
> The vision-spirit of the ship,
> The secret of his broken will.
>
> Beneath the pines he piped and swayed,
> Master of passion and of power;
> He was his soul and what he played,
> Immortal for a happy hour.
>
> He, singing into nature's heart,
> Guiding his will by the world's will,
> With deep, unconscious, childlike art
> Had sung his soul out and was still.

The triumph of the piper's art, a synthesis mingling the "vision-spirit of the ship" —the inspiration found in tradition, in the company of the mighty dead—and the "secret of his broken will"—the piper's surrender to the spirit of place, to what Scott calls "nature's heart" and "the world's will"—leads, interestingly enough, to death and silence. In the long and beautiful conclusion to the poem the ship returns to gather the piper unto itself, but then, for no natural reason, sinks to a cold dream-kingdom of art under the sea. The piper and the "dreaming crew" suffer a sea-change and become like jewels.

The piper succeeds in finding his place within the great tradition, but the strain costs him his life. Only in dream or death, it seems, can the two worlds be joined. Is this a parable of the impossible situation of the lonely colonial poet? The ambience seems vaguely Scottish, but it is also very generalized and symbolic; certainly Arll is a place of loneliness and isolation. And the poem provides our most vivid poetic expression of the alienation of the artist before A.M. Klein's "Portrait of the Poet as Landscape."

Scott is concerned as well with disparate worlds within Canada. In "The Height of Land" he seeks a point of balance between the imposed civilization and the wilderness, and also between two aspects of the wilderness: serenity and violence. They may also be seen, because the Canadian space opens one's mind to awareness of the cosmos, as two aspects of the universe. Like Roberts, Scott seeks a vantage point, climbing from "level to level" and sensing the "gathering of the waters in their sources." The poet "wrapped in his mantle on the height of land" for a moment sees that life is "as simple as to the shepherd seems his flock: / A Something to be guided by ideals—/ That in themselves are simple and serene." But this happy vision evoking, as "The Piper" does, a shepherd-poet gives way to another:

> The last weird lakelet foul with weedy growths
> And slimy viscid things the spirit loathes,
> Skin of vile water over viler mud
> Where the paddle stirred unutterable stenches,
> And the canoes seemed heavy with fear,
> Not to be urged toward the fatal shore
> Where a bush fire, smouldering, with sudden roar
> Leaped on a cedar and smothered it with light
> And terror. It had left the portage-height
> A tangle of slanted spruces burned to the roots,
> Covered still with patches of bright fire
> Smoking with incense of the fragrant resin
> That even then began to thin and lessen

> Into the gloom and glimmer of ruin.
> 'Tis overpast. How strange the stars have grown;
> The presage of extinction glows on their crests
> And they are beautied with impermanence;
> They shall be after the race of men
> And mourn for them who snared their fiery pinions
> Entangled in the meshes of bright words.

Everthing is doomed and impermanent, he sees, even the stars that will outlive the poets who write of them. An image early in the poem of "flakes of ash that play / At being moths, and flutter away / To fall in the dark and die as ashes" contains this theme in miniature. But the poet's determined mood of optimism is reinforced by the beauty of the sunrise and, before that, by the mystical sense of "Something" that "comes by flashes," casting a "spell / Golden and inappellable." This is possibly a literal reference to the northern lights, since Scott customarily speaks of the spiritual as it is manifested in natural phenomena, fusing idea and image immediately.

Unlike Roberts, Scott ponders the meaning of the "long view" afforded by his height of land. He reaches only tentative conclusions, however, and ends his meditation (as Yeats, another transitional poet, often does) with a question. Will the vision of simple ideals, "noble deed and noble thought immingled," seem as uncouth to the poet of the future as do cave-drawings to the modern Christian? Later poets—Al Purdy, Margaret Atwood, and others—have a different idea of the relative importance of "primitive" art and Christianity, but Scott, like Pratt after him, seems to cling to a Christian view of evolution and history. Will the dialectic of resolved opposites continue and progress forever? Or will the poet of the future see the world essentially as Scott sees it? Will man always greet the mystery of the world, "the deep / influx of spirit," with rapt wonder? Scott's two possibilities are not mutually exclusive, if one imagines that there will always be more mystery, more to be known. Like Roberts, Scott is determined to take an optimistic view of things, but he cannot ignore what he calls "the beauty of terror."

When you fish for the glory, you hook the darkness too. Sheila Watson's saying from *The Double Hook*, may be applied to the way a number of Canadian writers see the world; for Scott, reality is decidedly double-edged:

> all my spirit's sphere,
> Grows one half brightness and the other dead,
> One half all joy, the other vague alarms;
> And, holding each the other half in fee,
> Floats like the growing moon

> That bears implicitly
> Her lessening pearl of shadow
> Clasped in the crescent silver of her arms.
>
> "By a Child's Bed"

The poet searches for a synthesis, but it is not, it seems, to be found in this world.

Scott's personal and professional interest in Indians provides him with an effective means of dramatizing his vision of conflict. He sees the destruction or corruption of the Indian culture as a tragic result of the intrusion of old-world mores into the wilderness. The clash of cultures accompanies the ongoing conflict within nature itself.

In "On the Way to the Mission," one of Scott's most economical and successful poems, an Indian trapper with a toboggan apparently heaped high with furs is followed and killed by white men:

> They dogged him all one afternoon,
> Through the bright snow,
> Two whitemen servants of greed;
> He knew that they were there,
> But he turned not his head;
> He was an Indian trapper;
> He planted his snow-shoes firmly,
> He dragged the long toboggan
> Without rest.
>
> The three figures drifted
> Like shadows in the mind of a seer;
> The snow-shoes were whisperers
> On the threshold of awe.

The last four lines have a distancing effect, like a long shot in a film that reduces the actors to tiny dots on a white plane. The action of the poem is placed in a spiritual or imaginative context that somehow contains the physical one. The violent events that follow are held in the mind of the poet-seer; they are held at a certain distance so that they seem a point of local disturbance within a wider calm. The effect is later reinforced by the movement from straightforward, even terse, free-verse narrative to the rhyming quatrains that conclude the poem:

> They were the servants of greed;
> When the moon grew brighter

And the spruces were dark with sleep,
They shot him.
When he fell on a shield of moonlight
One of his arms clung to his burden;
The snow was not melted:
The spirit passed away.

Then the servants of greed
Tore off the cover to count their gains;
They shuddered away, into the shadows,
Hearing each the loud heart of the other.
Silence was born.

There in the tender moonlight,
As sweet as they were in life,
Glimmered the ivory features
Of the Indian's wife.

In the manner of the Montagnais women
Her hair was rolled with braid;
Under her waxen fingers
A crucifix was laid.

and so on for two more serene quatrains. The violence is not minimized, but the concluding calm suggests that the Indian couple have attained an ultimate, inviolate peace. In the sense that their stoic native dignity is unimpaired and unassailable, this might be true. But if it is an otherworldly beauty in death that is to be their reward, then it seems cold comfort indeed. It is presumably an *unintended* irony that these Indians have been converted to the religion of those who are victimizing and exploiting them. But one can argue that Scott, whose sympathy for the Indians is beyond question, nevertheless takes the side of the oppressors by insisting on an ultimate peace that is not of this world. As an important official in Indian Affairs until 1932, he seems to have believed fatalistically that assimilation and destruction of the Indian culture were inevitable.

In "On the Way to the Mission" and "The Forsaken" Scott demonstrates a sensitivity quite absent in his colleagues to the way in which short lines and a terse, free rhythm can convey the rugged quality of the Canadian environment:

All the lake-surface
Streamed with the hissing
Of millions of ice-flakes

Hurled by the wind;
Behind her the round
Of a lonely island
Roared like a fire
With the voice of the storm
In the deeps of the cedars.
Valiant, unshaken,
She took of her own flesh,
Baited the fish-hook,
Drew in a grey-trout,
Drew in his fellows,
Heaped them beside her,
Dead in the snow.
Valiant, unshaken,
She faced the long distance,
Wolf-haunted and lonely.

"The Forsaken"

This antedates by about twenty years the modernism of F.R. Scott, A.J.M. Smith and Dorothy Livesay. The poem that one wants to set beside "The Forsaken" is Smith's "The Lonely Land." It is probably just, then, that Smith has written the most perceptive essay so far on the poems of D.C. Scott.[1] In spite of the self-conscious rebellion of the poets of the 1920's against their predecessors, there is more continuity in the development of Canadian poetry than our literary historians have always supposed. But I will return to this theme later.

Scott has a greater technical virtuosity as well as more insight than the other Confederation poets, partly, one supposes, because of his interest in musical structures and a natural symbolism (as in "The Height of Land"), and partly because he saw more of his country and more of its wilder aspect. He saw the necessity of considering which of the poetic modes known to him might best express the spirit of the place and was thus more interested in formal experiment than the others.

The laconic, matter-of-fact presentation of the Canadian reality avoids a mellifluous pseudo-Wordsworthian sentimentalizing that is inappropriate to it. It is a pity, then, that "The Forsaken" has a somewhat tacked-on ending involving an insistence on a divine peace, "a silence deeper than silence," that seems unwarranted by the stark narrative and evocation of the wilderness that went before. The ending is reinforced, however, by the beautiful image of the old woman's breath persisting under the snow that covers her. In "On the Way to the Mission" the atmosphere of calm could be located in the mind of the seer or poet, which might perhaps partake of the divine mind, but here the matter is less subtly handled. Scott's insistence on an ultimate peace seems arbitrary, the result of wishful thinking if not complacency. The perfect peace of resolved opposites has to be taken on faith.

There is, on the other hand, one poem of Scott's that does not end in calm. This is "Powassan's Drum," one of his most perfectly realized achievements. Here Scott enters, with delicate music, the world of the Indian as memorably as Isabella Crawford does in "The Dark Stag."

> Stealthy as death the water
> Wanders in the long grass,
> And spangs of sunlight
> Slide on the slender reeds
> Like beads of bright oil.
> The sky is a bubble blown so tense
> The blue has gone grey
> Stretched to the throb-throb-throb-throb
> Throbbing of Powassan's Drum.
>
> It is a memory of hated things dead
> That he beats—famished—
> Or a menace of hated things to come
> That he beats—parched with anger
> And famished with hatred—?

The hatred of Powassan the medicine man is given no object in the poem, but a terrible frustration is expressed in his magic. Powassan conjures up a powerful Indian canoeist whose hand trails his own severed head through the water:

> The face looks through the water
> Up to its throne on the shoulders of power,
> Unquenched eyes burning in the water,
> Piercing beyond the shoulders of power
> Up to the fingers of the storm cloud.
> Is this the meaning of the magic—
> The translation into sight
> Of the viewless hate?

The answer would seem to be yes, but the vision sinks into the water as a murderous storm breaks. There is no after-calm in this poem. Here, Scott seems fully aware of the resentment and hatred felt by the Indian for the forces destroying his world. His magic is insufficient to prevent the tragedy. On another, more universal plane the headless Indian might also suggest primitive instinct separated from reason, a condition of psychic division that afflicts the human species in general. But the ferocity of Indian hatred seems the paramount theme: the poem is located within the Indian world. No resolution of the kind suggested in other Scott poems is attempted here.

Concern for the historical injustice done to the Indian occupies an important place in more recent Canadian writing. One need think only of Rudy Wiebe's recent novel *The Temptations of Big Bear*, or Peter Such's *Riverrun* about the Beothuks. The destruction of the Indian magic and its possible resurrection is a theme in Leonard Cohen's *Beautiful Losers*. Poets Purdy, Newlove, Acorn, Bissett, and Atwood pursue an Indian vision of the world. And the new accounts of Riel by Don Gutteridge and others reflect an interest in the half-way house of the métis. Decades before, Howard O'Hagan had suggested something of the beauty and the terror of the wild in his account of the haunting legend of a half-breed, *Tay John*—a man at home with neither people, only with the earth. In Margaret Laurence's most recent novel, *The Diviners*, the agent of a possible reconciliation between the races and a future fulfilment of all their dreams is Pique Tonnerre Gunn (or Gunn Tonnerre) who is Scottish, French, and Indian. More a symbol than a fully realized character, she is destined to inherit the stories and the significant objects—the Currie plaid pin and the knife which figured in *The Stone Angel*—of both Scots and métis. The Scots too, one remembers, have been persecuted and deprived in their time, as have the métis, and have lived in a primitive, rugged land. Pique's determination to recover her Indian heritage provides a moving conclusion to the story of her "Black Celt" mother, Morag. The myths of both peoples contribute to her being.

Scott's half-breed girls are decidedly less fortunate. Their intimations of wholeness are inchoate. They are haunted by their lost ancestors:

> A voice calls from the rapids,
> Deep, careless and free,
> A voice that is larger than her life
> Or than her death shall be.
>
> She covers her face with her blanket,
> Her fierce soul hates her breath,
> As it cries with a sudden passion
> For life or death.
>
> "The Half-Breed Girl"

A half-life, "living and partly living": this is the fate of Scott's half-breeds. This girl is, as it happens, half-Scottish. The reader is reminded that both the Europeans living in Canada and the Indians have lost their bearings and are wandering in limbo. The white man has deprived the Indian materially and spiritually, but he has also deprived himself. In a sense all Canadians live between two worlds and two cultures, one partly lost and one partly apprehended. The ultimate result is unforseeable.

A blind attempt at synthesis is made by another half-breed girl, Keejigo, in "At Gull Lake," a poem we may regard as the complex orchestration of all Scott's themes and motifs. Keejigo, third wife of Tabashaw, chief of the Saulteaux, offers herself to a trader, Nairne of the Orkneys. She is troubled "by fugitive visions" and intimations of a life larger than her own. Scott makes it clear as well that she embodies the land itself in its two aspects:

> The echoes of echo,
> Star she was named for
> Keejigo, star of the morning,
> Voices of storm—
> Wind-rush and lightning—
> The beauty of terror;
> The twilight moon
> Coloured like a prairie lily,
> The round moon of pure snow,
> The beauty of peace;
> Premonitions of love and of beauty
> Vague as shadows cast by a shadow.

Keejigo, star of the morning, is—in classical terms—a Venus figure, but she is powerless. In a beautiful poem within the poem she describes herself as a trapped and wounded animal. Instinctively she seeks release in offering herself with "abject unreasoning passion" to Nairne. But the trader, "a whiteman servant of greed," is unable to respond to the fierce spirit of place embodied in the barbarously beautiful girl, her dark face streaked with bright colours, and instead he cries, "Drive this bitch back to her master," as a storm rises. Caught between two worlds, the half-breed girl is rejected by both. Tabashaw blinds her with a live brand, and the old wives throw her over the lake bank like "a dead dog." Then the storm breaks. But the "beauty of terror" is followed by the "beauty of peace":

> The wind withdrew the veil from the shrine of the
>   moon,
> She rose changing her dusky shade for the glow

Of the prairie lily, till free of all blemish of colour
She came to her zenith without a cloud or a star,
A lovely perfection, snow-pure in the heaven of
    midnight.
After the beauty of terror the beauty of peace.

But Keejigo came no more to the camps of her people;
Only the midnight moon knew where she felt her way,
Only the leaves of autumn, the snows of winter
Knew where she lay.

Keejigo seems to persist as the still unheeded spirit of the land. But this is a thoroughly ambiguous apotheosis. On the literal plane we cannot even be sure if she is living or dead. On the symbolic plane the image of the white moon freed "of all blemish of colour" takes on a somewhat sinister and, presumably unintended, racist character if one assumes it is a picture of Keejigo perfected in death. There is definitely not here the irony that accompanies the more overt blanching of Catherine Tekakwitha in *Beautiful Losers*. If white is intended to signify perfection in death, then Keejigo's triumph is like that of the piper, possible only in another, purer world.

Scott's fatalism limits his insight into the Canadian condition; his religion apparently inclines him to refer (or defer) the more creative and potentially progressive possibilities of the Canadian situation to another world, or at least to the distant future. In this way he can have his overriding peace and his violence too. Still, he articulates more fully than the other poets the tensions inherent in the Canadian experience, especially in his depiction of half-breeds living between two worlds. It is a situation we are perhaps only beginning to leave behind.

Notes

1. A.J.M. Smith, *Towards a View of Canadian Letters: Selected Critical Essays 1928-1971* (Vancouver: University of British Columbia Press, 1973). Stanley Dragland's Ph.D. thesis, "Forms of the Imagination in the Poetry of Duncan Campbell Scott" (Queen's University, 1971), is also very good.

Weather

E.J. Pratt

E.J. Pratt set out, apparently quite deliberately, to be Canada's national poet. Since his leaning was to narrative (enlarging, whether consciously or not, upon Lampman's and Scott's briefer narratives), and to epic and adventures at sea, he may fairly be regarded as Canada's Whitman and her Melville in one person. Like Whitman, he combined a national vision with a sense of man's place in the universe at large. It is this larger vision, the Canadian "long view," that informs his best work.

Like the D.C. Scott of "The Height of Land," Pratt is concerned with the course of evolution and with what meaning the development of man may have. This was, of course, the concern of a number of Victorian poets—particularly Tennyson—but in Canada it is felt immediately in terms of the engagement with the environment, the vast Canadian space. This is evident in Pratt's major narratives. In his shorter poems of cosmic import, "The Highway" and "The Truant," Canada is not specified.

Star, rose, and Christ are the highly traditional symbolic landmarks along the poet's evolutionary highway; these are the perfect organizations of the inorganic, the organic, and the human, the informing principle in each case being love. For the Christian poet, as for Teilhard de Chardin, Christ symbolizes the ultimate goal of evolution and of human development, but man, in the twentieth century after the vision came to him, has yet fallen very short of this perfection. This is the burden of "The Highway," one of Pratt's most significant and revealing poems. The first star anticipated Christ, since it represented perfection; appropriately, a star announces his actual coming. The first rose, the first garden suggest Eden, Dante's multifoliate rose, paradise, and Christ at once. The simplest of images have great resonance here because of their traditional cultural and mythic associations in the West.

But what is one to make of the "cosmic seneschal" (or "marshal") who sets all this activity in motion in Pratt's poem? Is this medieval personage to be taken any more seriously as an image of God, or of the divine principle that realizes itself through evolution, than the pompous "great Panjandrum" of "The Truant"? What is a "seneschal" doing, even as a metaphor, in a poem about evolution and the "blossoming" of man as Christ? The notion of the universe as a medieval court presided over by a tyrant and, for that matter, the notion of a *linear* "highway" seem to be somewhat inconsistent with the vision of a universe unfolding almost as it should. Of course, "highway" is a pun; and both seneschal and marshal are servants, presumably here servants of evolution. But the notion of a feudal court is invoked by the use of these latter terms, and one is led to suspect that this is the same cosmic court ridiculed so exuberantly in "The Truant."

One can at least speculate, considering this diction, that Pratt the professed Christian is not very fond of God the Father, and may, indeed—in "The Truant" especially—be echoing the Romantic myth of Blake and Shelley that depicts Christ as a Promethean rebel against the unjust God of the Old Testament. D.G. Jones suggests in *Butterfly on Rock* that the Great Panjandrum is a *parody* of the god of Job, that is, a limited and limiting human conception rather than something awe-inspiring and ultimately mysterious.

"The Truant," often called Pratt's greatest poem, is a kind of new testament for the poet. A traditional notion of God—effectively summed up by Blake in the personage of "Old Nobodaddy," that whitebearded dotard snoozing in the clouds or else capriciously torturing his creatures—has, it seems, got to go. Instead, there is the alternate image conjured up by the title of a recent English novel by Yvonne Mitchell, *God Is Inexperienced* (1974). God may need help. Or, to put it another way, God is evolving too—through man and his developing consciousness. Certainly, the conception of God, that "Supreme Fiction," is evolving. But more than that, perhaps God is always potential, a wholeness that realizes itself more and more through the developing universe, most recently through man. Men are, so to speak, God's imperfectly tuned antennae. Such at any rate are the speculations stimulated in this reader by the poem. If this is indeed Pratt's view, then his Christ is not so much an historical figure as an image of man's potential future. (He speaks neither of the trinity nor of an afterlife.) The poet's Christianity may then be seen as humanistic, not traditional.

Carl Jung writes of the god of evolution in his *Memories, Dreams, Reflections*:

If the Creator were conscious of Himself, He would not need conscious creatures; nor is it probable that the extremely indirect methods of creation, which squander millions of years upon the development of countless species and creatures, are the outcome of purposeful intention. Natural history tells us of a haphazard and casual transformation of species over hundreds and millions of years of devouring and being devoured. The biological and political history of man is an elaborate repetition of the same thing. But the history of the mind offers a different picture. Here the miracle of reflecting consciousness intervenes—the second cosmogony.[1]

Such speculation leaves many questions unanswered, and possibly unanswerable. But is is significant that Jung goes on to speak of the development of human consciousness as constituting the only meaning to be found "within all the monstrous, apparently senseless biological turmoil" of past and present. Surely the author of "The Great Feud" and "Brébeuf and His Brethren" has similar concerns, whether he subscribes to any of Jung's theories or not. He writes of "human speech curved back upon itself / Through Druid runways and the Piltdown scarps, / Beyond the stammers of the Java caves, / To find its origins in hieroglyphs / On mouths and eyes and cheeks" ("Come Away, Death"). His mind moves away

> back before the emergence of fur or feather, back to the
> unvocal sea and down deep where the darkness spills its
>   wash
> on the threshold of light, where the lids never close upon
>   the
> eyes, where the inhabitants slay in silence and are as
>   silently
> slain
>
>   "Silences"

and forward to the realized Christ. This is the Canadian "long view" again, with a specifically Christian slant on the old disparities between fact and dream, nature and culture.

"The Truant" is splendid in its invective. Pratt's verbal energy, the witty mixture of Miltonic and modern scientific diction, makes the poem an exhilarating experience. It is stirring in its expression of defiance against a god and a universe of pure unvaried mechanism. Such a concept of God is, Pratt seems to say, as childish and outmoded as the medieval court employed here to express it. Like Jupiter in Shelley's *Prometheus Unbound*, the tyrant will, Pratt writes, ultimately be overthrown. This may be a reference to the second law of thermodynamics, as D.G. Jones suggests. Or it may be the prediction of some future transformation and redemption of energy. Or is it both? Meanwhile, the Great Panjandrum is given his due; he imposes illness and death on man.

But man affirms his own values in his defiance:

> We who have learned to clench
> Our fists and raise our lightless sockets
> To morning skies after the midnight raids,
> Yet cocked our ears to bugles on the barricades,
> And in cathedral rubble found a way to quench
> A dying thirst within a Galilean valley—
> No! by the Rood, we will not join your ballet.

The cross is here the symbol of man's ability to impart meaning to existence through rationality as well as through self-sacrificial love. Pratt preserves a late-Victorian faith in the masculine rational intelligence, that which takes the measure of the universe, and in human altruism that seems, alas, impossible for a serious writer today.

It is apparent that cosmic fantasy—as in "The Truant"—seems to have appealed to Pratt just as much as realistic narrative, but it is for the latter that he is best known. These poems were popular in their time for the same reasons that certain poems by Kipling and Service were popular: they told rousing stories. But Pratt had deeper concerns, and a few critics, Northrop Frye, John Sutherland, and Sandra Djwa (in *The Evolutionary Vision*) among them, have probed them.

"The *Titanic*," "Brébeuf and His Brethren," and "Towards the Last Spike," his most ambitious large poems, work and rework the themes Pratt shares with his prose counterpart, novelist F.P. Grove. In "The *Titanic*," for instance, man learns the dangers of nature and machine alike; the supposedly unsinkable ship lures him into a foolish complacency until the iceberg sinks it. It is hubris to trust in the infallibility of the machine. Machines may be beneficial if used properly; when man is overly reliant on them, however, he loses his soul; when he turns them to savage purposes (as in war), they become like prehistoric animals. Nature—in the form of the iceberg—remains powerful and terrible. But even in disaster man may respond with Christian fortitude, sacrificing himself for others rather than scrambling for survival in abject animal terror. The sense of community triumphs even as the ship sinks. Indeed, this image has been used by other Canadian writers. Leacock's well-known *Mariposa Belle* and the spirit ship that receives D.C. Scott's piper also represent community: in each case community, the sense of "communion" among human beings, is affirmed as the ship sinks, but the modes differ, being tragic, comic and fantastic respectively.

Communion among men and thus with God is the value affirmed in "Brébeuf" too, whatever one thinks of Pratt's treatment of the Jesuit mission and the Indians they set out to convert. (If a response to Pratt's generally negative treatment of the Indians is required, probably it is provided indirectly in *Beautiful Losers*, which will be discussed later.) Pratt's Indians represent man in a state of regression; they are worse than animals, who kill only to eat or in self-defence, since their human intelligence (like that of the priests of the Inquisition, as Frank Scott has wittily pointed out) is employed in the devising of tortures for their enemies. Pratt's priests, by contrast, approach Christ in their willingness to sacrifice themselves for what they regard as the cause of Christ. The story is told with a great deal of authentic detail and description; some passages are fascinating, some are very tedious. A poet of fact, exhaustively piling detail upon detail, runs this risk. Moreover, both blank verse and involved syntax can become exceedingly monotonous as the journeys and fates of the various brethren are recounted at length. "The *Titanic*" was much tighter; the use of rhyme enabled the poet to combine neatness with drive.

"Towards the Last Spike," Pratt's last attempt at a major poem on Canada, is, unfortunately, even looser in organization than "Brébeuf," and less successful as verse, just as "Brébeuf" is less successful technically than "The *Titanic*." The building of the C.P.R. is a more difficult story to dramatize, as Pierre Berton and the CBC proved once again with their curious mixture of scenery, documentary, mountainside chat, and costume drama in 1974. Pratt begins, as he did in "Brébeuf," with an evocation of the spirit of the times, a rousing description of the march of that nineteenth-century science and technology which made it possible to unify British North America by means of a railway. Union required the line, he writes; communication and community are great themes in all of Pratt's work and in Canadian literature generally, as many critics have observed. And "It was the same world then as now, thirsting for power." Man's thirst for power is obviously an obsession with Pratt too, but this exuberant powerlust may, he feels, be harnessed to a moral purpose, to the service of the community.

The poem recounts the political battle between Blake and Macdonald, but also the battle between man and brute nature. In the parliamentary battle for the railroad there is an emphasis on language as creation, a medium of power in politics as in poetry; names and metaphors have a primitive transforming magic. There is here as well an implicit analogy between the politician and the unacknowledged legislator who turns history into myth. The battle with nature is seen as romance: man awakens and conquers the sleeping dragon of Canadian space. Van Horne is a Promethean figure who overcomes the passive resistance of brute nature in the same spirit in which the truant defied the Great Panjandrum. Human social values are once again affirmed—this time in a comic rather than a tragic vein—though not without some cost in human life.

Much of this material is interesting, but some of it defeats even Pratt's very considerable powers of ingenuity. The story of the Lady of British Columbia and her on-again off-again courtship by Sir John—a kind of poetic political cartoon—would work much better in pictures. Here it becomes tedious. And while Sir John is best treated as a comic figure, the cavalier reference to the Riel Rebellion as dancing spots in the prime minister's groggy eye is, on reflection, not so funny. The rebellion is passed over briefly in a comic episode in which Sir John gathers courage from the bottle. There is no suggestion that the execution may not have been the prime minister's finest hour—Riel's side of the story was not told in verse until Don Gutteridge—nor is there emphasis on the irony of the way in which the rebellion may have brought the railroad closer to completion. Instead, Pratt is content to celebrate the great achievement of rational man shaping his environment. Virtue and Victorian optimism triumph. I am suggesting, I suppose, that he (like F.P. Grove) is, in the themes and structure of his art, somewhat lopsided on the side of rational, masculine values. In both cases this may be seen in a certain heaviness of style. Neither are great writers; they are lumbering likeable dinosaurs in our Canadian fields. Most pioneers are like that.

Pratt celebrates Western Christian man. His poems display little appreciation of primitive or non-Western man, or of woman. This probably reflects the Anglo-Saxon cultural assumptions of the turn of the century. And yet, there were exceptions to the rule. Carman had at his best a feminine receptiveness to the mystery and beauty of the world; it is appropriate that he should impersonate Sappho. Lampman and D.C. Scott too felt the necessity of letting the world wash over them as, paradoxically, part of the process of self-realization and autonomy. Scott's appreciation of the Indian, the wild, and the female come together in the person of Keejigo. Later, many fine women poets from Dorothy Livesay on celebrate the female principle, and many male poets—notably Al Purdy—sometimes express it. This distinction assumes that there are two ways of addressing the world, whether they are called male and female, rational and reverential, or something else. Man can set out to conquer and define and delimit the world, as Pratt's and Grove's protagonists do, or he can assimilate it by accepting and taking it into himself. Both are parts of the creative process, not to mention the task of making a civilization in the wilderness, and it is axiomatic that the major artist is conscious of being— perhaps to a greater degree than other men and women, though not different in kind—psychologically androgynous.

Pratt was a formal conservative, but he had greater resources to draw on than, say, Charles Sangster, because he was exuberantly engaged with the machine age. He broke away from the genteel Romantic-Victorian poetic idiom, building a vigorous new poetry from the great parent tradition, applying the great Elizabethans and Romantics to the great Canadian spaces, employing a huge and varied vocabulary ranging from modern scientific terminology to traditional fustian, and taking, consciously or not, certain hints about the narrative of conflict from Lampman and Scott. He passed on this new vigour to Earle Birney, who developed, eventually, a much more flexible narrative mode, as well as a more pessimistic vision.

Pratt is, at his best, a very fine poet indeed; I happen to think that the shorter poems, particularly "Silences" and "The Truant," are more successful than the ambitious long narratives. Canada was rapidly in transition from pioneer to technological society; Grove and Pratt are the important writers of that time. They wrestled with facts and dreams, Europe and America, nature and culture, environment and machine, the Darwinian theory and the vision of a Utopian future. They carried the dialogue begun by Lampman, Scott, and others a stage further.

Notes

1. C.J. Jung, *Memories, Dreams, Reflections* (London: Fontana Books, 1967), p. 371.

PART TWO

Inner Weather: The Modernists

Cross-Drafts

The Modernists

The poets of the generation that was young in the 1920's brought us modernism. It was a mixed blessing. Pratt had appropriated the techniques and methods of past centuries and put them to the service of a Newfoundlander's original gusto. The younger poets—F.R. Scott, A.J.M. Smith, A.M. Klein, Dorothy Livesay, Leo Kennedy, W.W.E. Ross, Raymond Knister, Robert Finch, A.G. Bailey, Ralph Gustafson, R.G. Everson, John Glassco, Kenneth Leslie, Philip Child, L.A. MacKay, Arthur Stringer, Roy Daniells—apparently gave assent to Smith's dictum that Canadian poets ought to pay more attention to their position in time, less to their position in space. (The Canadian obsession with space is not so easily brushed aside, however, as poems by Scott, Gustafson, Everson, and Bailey show.) What this meant in practice was to pay attention to the new technical directions of current British and American poetry, particularly to the revival of a metaphysical poetry, to free verse, and to imagism. This new wave was not, happily, wholly an aberration from the development of a native poetic idiom. If Pound and Eliot, two of the fathers of the new poetry, rejected the new world, it is also evident that what they took with them to England was an evolving poetics that was native to North American. In Canada Duncan Campbell Scott could be seen to be considering the possibilities of free verse a generation before Smith wrote "The Lonely Land" and some years before Pound and Eliot developed their own methods.

Still, the more effusive followers and successors of the Confederation poets tended to the Romantic-fatuous, and Smith is very witty at their expense. Unfortunately, sometimes good but old-fashioned poets like Marjorie Pickthall and Wilson MacDonald became victims of the revolution as well. Ironically, a review of Smith's *Collected Poems* by an unsympathetic poet of the next generation, Lionel Kearns, sounds rather like Smith's own attacks on the decadent "maple-leaf" poets of his time.

Kearns accuses Smith of relying on the "time-worn gimmicks of traditional rhyme and regular metre, usually heavily iambic" and remarks that everything is "a kind of pastiche." Is this what is meant by poetic justice?[1] Certainly poets of Kearns's generation have carried the rejection of traditional modes and of some of their Canadian elders as far as did those same elders.

In similar fashion, but with greater zest, the young Smith lambasted the unfortunate successors of Roberts, Carman, Lampman and Scott:

> The bulk of Canadian verse is romantic in conception and conventional in form. Its two great themes are Nature and Love—nature humanized, endowed with feeling, and made sentimental; love idealized, sanctified, and inflated. Its characteristic type is the lyric. Its rhythms are definite, mechanically correct, and obvious; its rhymes are commonplace...the writers...are not interested in saying anything in particular; they merely wish to show that they are capable of turning out a number of regular stanzas in which statements are made about the writer's emotions, say "In Winter," or "At Montmorenci Falls," or "In a Birch Bark Canoe." Other exercises are concerned with pine trees, the open road, God, showshoes or Pan. The most popular experience is to be pained, hurt, stabbed or seared by Beauty—preferably by the yellow flame of a crocus in the spring or the red flame of a maple leaf in autumn.[2]
>
> The Canadian poet, if this kind of thing truly represents his feelings and his thoughts, is a half-baked, hyper-sensitive, poorly adjusted, and frequently neurotic individual that no one in his senses would trust to drive a car or light a furnace. He is the victim of his feelings and fancies, or of what he fancies his feelings ought to be, and his emotional aberrations are out of all proportion to the experience that brings them into being. He has a soft heart and a soft soul; and a soft head.[3]

What is interesting, in retrospect, about these amusing sallies is their (admittedly limited) application to Smith's own work. After all, he writes of Pan, Canadian nature, and painful beauty too. "The most popular experience is to be pained, hurt, stabbed or seared by Beauty": might not this statement apply to "The Lonely Land," "Swift Current," "Sea-Cliff," "To Hold in a Poem," "In the Wilderness," and "To the Haggard Moon"? To be sure, Smith is less present in his work and more objective than Carman, who seems to be the ultimate target of his attack, but the subject matter and implicit sense of desolation are akin to those of Carman's melancholy utterance. Is one inclined to trust the author of intricate mythological or "literary" poems such as "Like an Old Proud King in a Parable," "The Plot against Proteus," "Choros," "Ode: the Eumenides," and "To Henry Vaughan" to be able to drive a car or light a furnace? Come to think of it, the answer should probably be yes, given the complicated mechanics of some of the poems. Smith argues in his early essays that a modern poetry must reflect the modern reality, but the contemporary world does not get much of a show in all his cool classicizing. It is, one gathers, in his technique rather than his subject matter that Smith is modern. Rejecting the possibility of a native poetry, he opts for an updated colonialism when he derives his technique from Yeats, Eliot, and the Sitwells. Eliot could be of some use in the development of a native poetic idiom—though not so helpful, as Smith may unconsciously have recognized when he wrote "The Lonely Land," as D.C. Scott—but Yeats and the Sitwells are hopelessly European. Moreover, among modernist poets from any country, Smith is, most of the time, a formal conservative, as Lionel Kearns pointed out.

All that said, it remains true that Smith and the other poets of his generation brought a new sophistication and technical intelligence to Canadian poetry. This was certainly of some value—if not an end in itself, as it seems to be in some of Smith's poems—to those later poets who *did* develop a native idiom (for example, Al Purdy), just as the more recent invasion in the 1960's of "Black Mountain" and other theories from the United States, delivered unto us by a second wave of colonized Canadian technicians and metaphysicians, has been of some use. Moreover, Arthur Smith has written excellent poems, surely justification enough of any man's lifework. The best are the imagist nature poems, especially "The Lonely Land," which are verbal counterparts to the paintings of the Group of Seven, though they are a good deal less colourful—Carman and D.C. Scott are closer to the Group in this respect—delicate and beautiful love poems like "Fields of Long Grass," and the poems about death, particularly, "Prothalamium," which is metaphysical in style and substance and yet wholly transcends pastiche:

> Now these are me, whose thought is mine, and hers,
> Who are alone here in this narrow room—
> Tree fumbling pane, bell tolling,
> Ceiling dripping and the plaster falling,
> And Death, the voluptuous, calling.

The homage to Webster, Shakespeare, and Donne; the references to the latter's conceit of incest in the grave after death and to his famous "No man is an island" passage; allusions to *Hamlet* and *The Duchess of Malfi*;

borrowed images of narrow crumbling room, tolling bell, dead tree, and Death the lover: all serve to convey a mingled horror and fascination with death that is obviously genuine and deeply personal to the poet. In fact, death is Arthur Smith's obsessive subject and major concern as a poet; it has inspired his simplest, must lucid and most personal poems, and in an involved and witty sonnet like "The Wisdom of Old Jelly-Roll" it adds a necessary dimension of "heart" to the wordplay. Smith's customary "cool"—expressed in his intricate formal designs—may itself be a response to and a defiance of the hard fact of mortality, but readers ought to be grateful that his cool is not always kept.

If, aside from this, Smith devotes himself mainly to myth and to earlier literature, F.R. Scott is usually his necessary complement: a poetic realist concerned with social problems and with the development of Canada. Son of a minor poet associated with the Confederation group, he shared in the oedipal rebellion of the 1920's, as his heavyhanded but delightful satire "The Canadian Authors Meet" indicates. And in "Overture" he declares that he cannot hear old music at a time when a new era is being born. His best poems convey a sense of pleasure and excitement in life in a new land as a new world dawns. Apparently a flexible free-verse line—though he does not employ it a great deal—comes more easily to Scott than to Smith; he is more at home in an idiom based on natural and colloquial speech. His imagist nature poems, like Smith's, express a feeling for the Canadian landscape as it often is, in all its coldness and harshness, not as it might be when infused with Wordsworthian sentiment. His satires expose a social system insufficiently attuned to human values. But his most memorable and, I suspect, most enduring poems are those in which his social and his natural observations are fused to present—as Pratt and D.C. Scott had before him and as Birney and Purdy would afterwards—a vision of Canada that attempts to define man's place in a vast and continuously evolving universe. These poems, then, particularly "Trans Canada," "Lakeshore," and "Laurentian Shield," are squarely within the Canadian poetic mainstream, whatever break the rebels of the 1920's thought that they were making.

"Lakeshore" begins with simple description of the lake's edge. But soon the poet is drawn to the underwater world in which fish, like planes, have free passage in all directions. He observes his own reflection and contemplates two worlds; the dry land of our present civilization and the world of our evolutionary past. Swimmers, he sees, are immersed in the race-memories of the collective unconscious. Other Canadian poets have made swimming and diving important symbolic activities. W.W.E. Ross, Dorothy Livesay, A.M. Klein, and Irving Layton all have significant swimming poems; probably Ross and Scott were there first, but Layton has carried the matter furthest. And Pratt explores the undersea world of our non-human ancestors. Men long, Scott suggests, to be amphibious again, but cannot be, though they strive as compensation and, in Scott's witty paradox, "with cold and fishy care" to "make an ocean of the air," to fly freely in a third world that resembles the first. The earth is a prison:

> This is our talent, to have grown
> Upright in posture, false-erect,
> A landed gentry, circumspect,
> Tied to a horizontal soil
> The floor and ceiling of the soul.

The phrase "landed gentry" is a double entendre, typical of Scott; it refers presumably to our capitalist acquisitiveness and mania for property and at the same time to our stranded biological and spiritual condition. Yet to have been held to the water would also have been an imprisonment; the poem is ambivalent about the possibility of freedom. Scott concludes:

> Sometimes, upon a crowded street,
> I feel the sudden rain come down
> And in the old, magnetic sound
> I hear the opening of a gate
> That loosens all the seven seas.
> Watching the whole creation drown
> I muse, alone, on Ararat.

Suddenly, the poet is Noah on his mountain. Throughout the poem there has been reference to passageways—doorways, colonnades, and gates. Now a new opening spells flood and disaster for "the whole creation." In this apparent reversal the watery world is a trap, not a liberation. Since the poet survives, however, on his height of land, it appears that modern capitalist civilization (and, more than that, the biological and evolutionary development that has produced it) is drowned spiritually, not literally. Only the lonely poet has a larger vision.

The poem is spare and elegant in the best "modernist" way; it is also complex and ambivalent (in the best "Canadian" way) about the possible meaning of man's successive passages from world to world. Is this progression or regression? Or both at once? Scott's liberal optimism seems to be tempered by a lingering sense of the Fall and of man's incorrigible nature. In "Trans Canada" he writes:

> Man, the lofty worm, tunnels his latest clay,
> And bores his new career.

Even here, as he conquers the second "ocean of the air" and sets forth on "the road to suns," man remains a boring earthworm in the vast, unhuman emptiness. But Scott preserves an ironic tone; he does not develop the full-blown pessimism of an Earle Birney.

In "Laurentian Shield" Scott expresses both dismay and hope. Like Pratt, he sees the reasoned order of language as analogous to the order that human settlement and exploitation impose on nature:

> Now there are pre-words,
> Cabin syllables,
> Nouns of settlement
> Slowly forming, with steel syntax,
> The long sentence of its exploitation.

The "steel syntax" is the railway; the word "sentence" refers both to language and to the imposition of man's will (as in a court of law) on the environment. The land is "sentenced" to exploitation by hunters, miners and the "bold commands of monopoly." But the future must involve more than mere economic growth; human values must be affirmed:

> a deeper note is sounding, heard in the mines,
> The scattered camps and the mills, a language of life,
> And what will be written in the full culture of
>   occupation
> Will come, presently, tomorrow,
> From millions whose hands can turn this rock into
>   children.

This is vague but hopeful. Scott is generally a liberal optimist, like Pratt, despite his sense of what is wrong both with man and with Canadian society. But there is a subtle irony and a certain ambivalence in his most serious work—qualities he shares with more ambitious and more prolific Canadian writers.

Ralph Gustafson has also written of the Canadian reality, though much of his highly accomplished work is, like Smith's, based on things mythological and literary, and much has to do with travel and works of art. An internationalist like Smith and John Glassco, Gustafson has nevertheless given us his Rocky Mountain poems and a few others on Canadian subjects. There is, of course, no reason why a Canadian might not write great poems, none of which had any specific reference to Canada. He would still be recognizably Canadian, though, or he could not be authentic:

perhaps Alain Grandbois, with his great sense of cosmic space, is a French-Canadian example of this. Nevertheless, I have no doubt that Gustafson's "Canadian" poems are his most appealing and accessible. He is a difficult poet, not because, as some have said, his work is excessively cerebral—it is in fact highly sensuous—but because it is very dense and compressed. Intricate sound effects and elliptical syntax carry a train of thought that has more to do with one man's immediate intellectual and sensuous response to the world than with the elaboration of any very startling or original philosophy. Gustafson is both painter and musician in words. This technical sophistication has its own delights, but the poem is not always to be grasped immediately. Perhaps it is because the physical reality of the mountains is sufficiently overwhelming that the poems about them communicate more directly and easily than the European poems to the grateful reader. The poet's natural tendency to compression is encouraged by a European work of art, but the great spaces evoke a more straight-forward response:

> In Europe, you can't move without going down into history.
> Here, all is a beginning. I saw a salmon jump
> Again and again, against the current,
> The timbered hills a background, wooded green
> Uprushed through; the salmon jumped, silver.

Gustafson, like Scott, enjoys the world. Though he broods about death as Smith does and sometimes catalogues life's horrors, he responds with wonder and delight to the world's beauty, sometimes very simply and directly.

John Glassco is a more sombre poet. Elegiac, elegant, ruminative, he has been to school to Wordsworth, Frost and Eliot. Transience, void, loss, the terrible ennui when the vision of beauty and wonder has faded, these are his subjects. His dying Don Quixote declares:

> Oh my God
> I have lost everything
> In the calm of my sanity
> Like a tree which regards itself
> In still water
> Seeing only another tree,
> Not as when the crazy winds of heaven blew
> Turning it to a perpetual fountain
> Of shaken leaves.

This is beautiful and deeply moving, as much of Glassco's poetry is. His is a small but very distinguished body of work, like Scott's and Smith's.

Much more could be said about all of the poets of this generation (about, for instance, A.G. Bailey, who has something of Gustafson's compression as well as a strong feeling for the stories, myths, animals and landscapes of eastern Canada); they deserve a whole book. There are obvious family resemblances among them, even though each is distinctive. Smith, Gustafson, Glassco, and Robert Finch are elegant, erudite, and witty; Scott, Ross, Knister, Bailey and (sometimes) Gustafson more "Canadian" in the obvious sense of the word. But all aim for a technical sophistication that avoids the obvious. In Klein's words, "How they do fear the slap of the flat of the platitude!" The dangers run by such poetry, as Klein also notes, are those of obscurity and triviality. It is fair to say that the latter is usually avoided, but a good proportion of the work of these fine poets—miniaturists or technicians all—can be called obscure and might even be labelled by those who desire a large Canadian utterance, comparable to Whitman's poetry of America, irrelevant. This is, of course, somewhat unfair, but understandable. Technique can be a garrison too.

Two poets of this time have undergone rather more development in the direction of a more open form than the others. These are R.G. Everson and Dorothy Livesay. I suppose Everson belongs, like Ross and Knister, in the imagist wing of modernism, but his vision is larger. He is a thoughtful poet who likes to comment on everything under the sun in free-ish verse. Generally he is affirmative and life-loving like Gustafson; he writes of people—births, deaths, loves—more than of art, though. The poems give the impression, true or not, that Everson has lived in all parts of Canada and likes them equally. Like Al Purdy, he brings far and near, large and small together:

> Out this cabin window
> stars of the Milky Way appear together
> If we get there
> likely all worlds will be far from one another
>
> though I have heard constellations colliding in Lyra
>
> Our washrooms are connected underground
>
> "How wonderful to hear that human sound"

There are no spectacular effects in Everson's poetry, but he has, again like Al Purdy, developed a colloquial style and a vocal rhythm flexible enough that he can write about anything that takes his wandering fancy. This is—because natural to the man speaking in Canada—a Canadian idiom.

Dorothy Livesay has been somewhat more ambitious than Everson. She is, except for the characteristic delicacy that provides a context for her occasional and deliberate coarseness, the original earth-mother of modern Canadian poetry. In the brief foreword to her *Collected Poems: The Two Seasons* she writes, "Perhaps we are a country more feminine than we like to admit, because the unifying, regenerative principle is a passion with us." Her work, can be read, then, as a corrective to the rational masculine bias of many of the earlier writers and as an exploration of the female nature of Canada and the Canadian psychology. In the poems engendered by sixty-odd years of living she plays the role of earth-mother enthusiastically.

Livesay also states in her "Foreword": "I note the dichotomy that exists here between town and country—that pull between community and private identity that is characteristic of being a woman; and characteristic, for that matter, of life 'north,' life in Canada." This speaks to me of a dual psychic rhythm that is Canadian. The experience of town and country, the communal and the individual, summer and winter, withdrawal and return can give us that flexible, shifting perspective.

Livesay's early poems are brief imagist lyrics—sometimes free, sometimes rhymed and metrical. Their subjects are love, houses, greenery, the weather. These are poems of innocence; they seem deliberately naive. But one of them, "Green Rain," is haunting in its evocation of woman and landscape:

> I remember long veils of green rain
> Feathered like the shawl of my grandmother—
> Green from the half-green of the spring trees
> Waving in the valley.

> I remember the road
> Like the one which leads to my grandmother's house,
> A warm house, with green carpets,
> Geraniums, a trilling canary
> And shining horse-hair chairs;
> And the silence, full of the rain's falling
> Was like my grandmother's parlour
> Alive with herself and her voice, rising and falling—
> Rain and wind intermingled.

> I remember on that day
> I was thinking only of my love
> And of my love's house.
> But now I remember the day
> As I remember my grandmother.
> I remember the rain as the feathery fringe of her shawl.

How cunningly the notion of the alterations of memory is introduced: the rain becomes green because the trees were beginning to be green, and it is now associated with grandmother's shawl. The reader is then deflected from the road that only *resembles* the road to grandmother to grandmother's house itself. At the time, the speaker of the poem was full of the thought of her love and was presumably going through the rain to see him at his house, but in retrospect it is her grandmother who remains important and who is associated in her mind with this time and place. Woman and environment are identified as the rain becomes the fringe of the woman's shawl, and the woman comes to represent the spirit of the land for the poet. Thus we inhabit our ancestors and spiritual forebears as they inhabit us; a later woman poet, Margaret Atwood, suggests this as well in "The Settlers" and *The Journals of Susanna Moodie.* These ancestors are men, too, of course—Al Purdy's *In Search of Owen Roblin* provides an example—but it seems appropriate to think of the land as feminine, because open space and enduring earth are female symbols. This helps to account for all our representative literary matriarchs and grandmothers (frequently fierce, as befits Canada): Ellen making a spatial pattern of history in *The Mountain and the Valley*, Susanna Moodie, Hagar Shipley, old Mrs. Potter in *The Double Hook,* obstreperous Gran in *Jalna.*

Livesay did not rest content with imagism but was moved by the events of the 1930's and 1940's to extend herself in the engagement with large social themes. This was an admirable response to urgent problems but also something of a digression from the poet's natural bent; long poems in blank verse and/or nursery-rhyme rhythms can become tedious or sententious. At least, a little of each goes a long way with me, which may explain in part why I am not overfond of Pratt's "Towards the Last Spike." Later social poets such as Milton Acorn, Raymond Souster, Pat Lane, and Tom Wayman have dealt effectively with the lives of the common people in a somewhat more economic fashion. But Livesay deserves all credit, with Frank Scott, for pioneering a social and socialist poetry in Canada. These poems display a human concern and an awareness of uncorrected injustice that were all too rare at the time.

In later phases of her long career Dorothy Livesay has grown remarkably as an artist. The very personal poems of the 1960's are increasingly tense and dramatic, and her latest poems of love, aging and the eternal connection with sun, earth and growing things show her at her best. At her most effective, in, for example, "Bartok and the Geranium," "Lorca," and "Lament," she has always displayed a considerable feel for tight patterns of sound, rhythm and symbol. She loves to create internal rhymes and sound effects ("Sun, stun me, sustain me"). In her most notable poems she is usually terse, laconic:

Yet in this room, this moment now
These together breathe and be:
She, essence of serenity,
He in a mad intensity
Soars beyond sight
Then hurls, lost Lucifer,
From heaven's height.
And when he's done, he's out:

She lays a lip against the glass
And preens herself in light.

"Bartok and the Geranium"

This is the poet's true and distinctive voice. Though she celebrates greenery
and fecundity throughout her work, she is by nature a delicate, spare writer,
and this may explain why the documentaries and blank-verse narratives,
well-written as they are, have a worked-up quality about them. They lack
the tightness, the high definition of the most authentic Livesay.

"Bartok and the Geranium" reveals the poet's attachment to the values
associated with the female principle—endurance, serenity, continuity,
affinity with the land and with natural process. Yet she does not slight the
male drive to the abstract and to the stars; it is given almost equal time in
the poem. Livesay's poems betray a sympathy for Man, even though
the mythic figure of Woman—she who simply *is* while he shoots his bolt,
intellectually and sexually, and then is "out"—is of primary importance to
her. On the realistic plane, these poems provide a very frank record of the
youth and maturity of a Canadian woman, a psychic autobiography, as
Livesay puts it, and they are remarkable and unique in Canadian literature
for that alone. Livesay was writing thus before (or, in the case of *The
Unquiet Bed,* simultaneously with) the American female poets of a
confessional persuasion, and she is certainly franker than such earlier
contemporaries as Edna St. Vincent Millay. She had Isabella Crawford,
with her mythic vision of the land, and Emily Dickinson, with her tough,
gnomic response to the world, to look back to, but she went forward to
articulate the life of a twentieth-century woman. This in turn looks forward
to the work of Waddington, Atwood, MacEwen and others and is the basis
for Dorothy Livesay's unique position among the poets of her own
generation. In her case modernism has meant more than eclectic
detachment.

Notes

1. *Canadian Literature* 36(1968): 67-68.
2. Dudek and Gnarowski, eds., *The Making of Modern Poetry in Canada* (Toronto: McGraw-Hill Ryerson, 1967), pp. 38-39.
3. Ibid., p. 39.

The nth Adam

A. M. Klein

Looked at from my view of what is Canadian, A. M. Klein becomes a key figure, as Malcolm Ross, whose basic insights I share and have learned from, observed long ago in his review of *The Second Scroll*.[1]

Klein was, in the late 1920's, associated with the "Montreal group" of Scott, Smith, and Kennedy, but his Jewishness gave him a somewhat different slant on things. It made him, paradoxically, more fully Canadian. The problems of the immigrant in the new land, the myriad-mindedness of Canadians taken as a whole, the multicultural nature of the new country, the problems of the visionary who exists in spiritual exile: these Canadian realities are illuminated in his work. Much has been written elsewhere of *The Second Scroll,* which is a Zionist fable. Still, it is worth noting that the utopian Israel of the novel bears little resemblance to the reality of today; the golden vision of the promised homeland remains compelling partly because it is, by analogy, relevant to the Canadian attempt to achieve community, and partly because WASPs and other Euro-Canadians carry around the mythical baggage of the Old Testament too. Indeed a dual allegiance splits Klein in two. His Uncle Melech gives himself wholly to Israel; his narrator belongs forever, despite his vicarious participation in Melech's passion, to the fabled city of Montreal. It is a thoroughly Canadian double-vision (indeed, on closer examination, a multiple-vision). Klein's overlapping allegiances are to a city, a people, the ideal of Zion, and the nation of Canada.

One finds in Klein's work Poland, Montreal, Canada, and Israel, folklore, Chassidism, law, geometry, socialism, Zionism, and Canadian nationalism, Arabs, Jews, Québécois, Indians, and poets. His world is truly multicultural, as Canada is. His use of language reflects, for better and for worse, a multilingualism like that of Vladimir Nabokov or of Klein's principal non-Jewish cultural hero, James Joyce.

I have said before that Klein was, in his early work, closeted, more precisely ghettoized. Like Heavysege, he looked to the past—in his case both to the Jewish past and to the world of the great Christian poets of Elizabethan England—evading the immediate reality of Montreal. He wanted, as he admitted, to live in an earlier century. But even this early verse is interesting for the light it sheds on the cultural fortress, or garrison, that a tightly knit immigrant group with ancient traditions could erect in the new world. Perhaps the pressure of alien Montreal is part of the genesis of these poems of embattled Jewry, just as Heavysege's biblical poems may reflect the pressure of Canadian nature, as Frye suggests, even though Montreal goes unmentioned.

Linguistic playfulness, an addiction to rhyme and a penchant for striking imagery characterize Klein's earliest work. A fondness for light verse—some of it juvenile, some of it delightful—is the counterpart to the more sombre accounts of Jewish suffering throughout the centuries. There are also a few poems which do suggest the modern urban world, but even here the poet's mind moves backward in time. In one of these, the delightful sonnet, "My Literati Friends in Restaurants," the polyglot poet scribbles the last line of the *Divine Comedy* on a menu and dreams of his love while his intellectual friends bicker and shout their abstract love for the working classes.

But most of the early work seems to me to be clumsy and fustian, sometimes because of the dangerous tactic of a deliberately archaic diction and syntax as a means of rendering the medieval and ancient Jewish world, sometimes because the rhymes are not subtle enough to lift the satires out of the realm of burlesque. This is a fault of much of the radical poetry, and it is at its worst in *The Hitleriad* of 1944. It was Whitman, I think, who said of Poe that he carried the rhyming art to excess, and it might be added of Klein that his technical strengths often become weaknesses through excess. One takes the bad with the good when a poet is as vital and exuberant as this.

When Klein's devices work, however, the result is a poetry of great originality. In *Hath Not a Jew*, where the best of the early work is collected Klein explores the situation of the Jews throughout history in a language adapted from that of Chaucer, Spenser, Shakespeare, Marlowe, and Milton. Like the Newfoundlander Pratt, he does not hesitate to borrow the extravagant gestures of the great poets of the English tradition: this is the Canadian eclecticism, the way in which Sangster, Heavysege, Crawford, Pratt, Smith, and the early Birney dealt with the anomalous Canadian condition. Surprisingly, the risk often pays off: much of Klein's hybrid verse—which unites the great but disparate traditions of English literature and Hebrew lore—is fresh, colourful, and scintillating, especially in poems for children based on Jewish folklore and Chassidic tales from Poland, the land of Klein's immediate ancestors. These are, of course, the simplest in form and thus the least ornate. There is, in this book, almost no reference to Canada or identifiable mention of Montreal. But one of the most impressive poems, "Out of the Pulver and the Polished Lens," develops a universal statement of the search for "identity" in terms of Baruch Spinoza's liberation from ghetto and synagogue into a wider world full of God's presence. The search for "God" is, the poet suggests, the search for one's fullest and not one's narrowest self, similar to Jung's notion of the individuation process. Such a concern transcends cultural barriers and fore- shadows Klein's later expressions of sympathy for French Canada.

In the radical poems, too, Klein extends his sympathy to all who suffer from economic injustice. These poems are somewhat hit and miss, but certainly there are among them, as Klein's Elizabethan predecessors might say, "palpable hits." Moreover, Klein's poems of social protest prepare the way for the fusion of private vision and public observation in *The Rocking Chair*. Meanwhile *Poems* (1944) continues his articulation of specifically Jewish concerns. In the poems that immediately precede *The Rocking Chair*, some of which were later employed as glosses in *The Second Scroll*, there is a new assurance, a gradual movement toward a more consistently modern idiom. What his most severe critics have regarded as a facility for empty rhetoric Klein turns to appropriate purposes.

The Rocking Chair is a landmark in the history of Canadian poetry. Stylistically, Klein has benefited from association with other Montreal poets of the 1940's (P.K. Page, the English poet Patrick Anderson, perhaps even the early Irving Layton) and from acquaintance with the work of Yeats, Hopkins, Auden, Thomas, and the American Karl Shapiro (he had already long shown evidence of an acquaintance with Eliot), but he remains very definitely himself, probably because his mastery of several languages brings an individuality, if not an oddity, to his manner of negotiating English. In a richly inventive, sometimes even ornate language he applies his considerable insight into the nature of minority groups to the French-Canadians, Canadians in general, Canadian Indians, and even the scattered tribe of Canadian poets. In this he expresses what must become the collective Canadian consciousness, a tapestry of minority groups, each in its own cultural garrison or ghetto and surrounded by a vast and forbidding landscape. "Portrait of the Poet As Landscape" is the key poem, for in it the poet's function is seen as the articulation of man's place in the social, natural, and cosmic landscape (though landscape is no longer the word), and of its life in him. Unfortunately, as the poem also indicates, hardly anyone was likely to be listening in 1948, and Klein was never able to enjoy an audience like that of the 1960's and 1970's, which has lionized his successors (Layton, Purdy, Cohen, Atwood, and so forth) for their enlargement upon these basic themes.

I have said that Klein's work reflects the Canadian multiculturalism, but he finds unity in all the diversity. In "The Provinces" he writes

> the heart seeks one, the heart, and also the mind
> seeks single the thing that makes them one, if one.

And in "Grain Elevator" all his worlds are yoked together in a cinematic flow of images flashing by at almost hallucinatory speed, a "montage/of inconsequent time and uncontiguous space" that binds a Montreal grain elevator to Babylon, Leviathan, the ark, Joseph's dreams in Egypt, Saskatchewan, the liberation of the Bastille, Araby, Mongolians in the steerage of a ship, and a number of other things, in fact to all times, places and peoples that have been sustained by bread. Recurrent images of prison, ship and river (the river of grain which itself encourages a kind of hallucination; the river of life) give way to the eventual flower-box (and flour-box) from and through which "all the coloured faces of mankind" are raised. Canada contains, in the microcosm of the grain elevator, a universe of need and its possible fulfilment. Material and imaginative liberation occur together in this utopian vision: it offers what Margaret Avison calls "jail-break/and re-creation." Exuberant metaphor articulates a basic human (and in other poems an extra-human) unity in diversity.

Here and in "Lone Bather" identity with the world is achieved through metamorphosis. Language is made an instrument of magic, a flexible, esemplastic substance. The swimmer becomes bird, dolphin, plant, and merman in turn. This poem is obviously kin to Frank Scott's "Lakeshore" and Irving Layton's "The Swimmer." Here Klein's customary dislocation of conventional syntax functions as part of the process by which the normal perception of reality is broken down in order to reveal man's kinship with all living things, a kinship that proves ultimately to be identity as he returns to his evolutionary origin:

> Upon the ecstatic diving board the diver,
> poised for parabolas, lets go
> lets go his manshape to become a bird.
> Is bird, and topsy-turvy
> the pool floats overhead, and the white tiles snow
> their crazy hexagons. Is dolphin. Then
> is plant with lilies bursting from his heels.

As the diver becomes a bird in the third line, a moment of beauty is caught in iambic pentameter; the poet shifts in and out of this metrical norm. The world is re-arranged and reconstituted; the reader is even allowed, by a sudden shift of perspective, a momentary look through the diver's eyes.

> Up, he is chipped enamel, grained with hair.
> The gloss of his footsteps follows him to the showers,
> the showers, and the male room, and the towel
> which rubs the bird, the plant, the dolphin back again
> personable plain.

Klein's magic is Canadian insofar as it proposes an ultimate unity while retaining a respect for the individual categories, cultures, boundaries, and creatures that make up the whole. He sympathizes deeply with most of his not-so-beautiful losers—the poets, Indians, Jews, librarians, habitants, filles majeures, hustlers, politicians and harassed businessmen who populate *The Rocking Chair*. At the same time they are all placed within the grand context of a divine, and human, comedy, the ongoing process of natural and human life. Klein is a poet with a central and universal mythic structure, in his case largely based in Cabbala, behind him—like Dante, Chaucer, Shakespeare, Milton, Yeats, Eliot, and the ancient poets. He sees himself as the nth Adam naming, indeed re-creating, the world as language. His is essentially a religious sensibility, and his great theme is the transcendence of evil through human sympathy.

To be a Canadian, Klein suggests, is to experience alienation and exile, to know cultural conflict as well as cultural diversity. All Canadians, in this view, are like wandering Jews in a vast and mysterious land of exile. (By now, many of us have begun to feel at home, but this happy process is far from complete.) It seems to me, as it did to Klein, advisable in this situation that the numerous Canadian garrisons attempt to communicate their hopes and anxieties to one another and to communicate also the attempts of each cultural or regional community to achieve some feeling of harmony with the land and, perhaps through the land, with a larger order of things in the universe. Thus art, thus the poet who takes into himself the landscape.

It was, then, potentially tragic that, at least at times, Klein saw the poet, once the acknowledged spokesman for his culture, as an invisible man hopelessly unable to communicate his essential vision to a society entangled in technology and drugged with its attendant, American, pop culture. The poet of "Portrait" holds his vision as a secret, harbouring in his situation of neglect feelings of profound ambivalence about his own worth and inclined to doubt even his own existence. Like David Canaan in Ernest Buckler's classic novel *The Mountain and the Valley*, Moses Klein was not destined to enter the promised land; Layton was the militant Joshua who did. Some poets, Klein writes, in a passage both humorous and sinister, "go mystical, and some go mad." The experience of divinity, of the wholeness of things, that moves man to artistic creation may, after all, he suggests, be just a form of madness. The serious artist may well be dismissed as a madman by a society that has forsaken any experience of transcendence.

But the poet is the man whose nature will not allow him to forgo the experience of wholeness, even if his merely individual ego be submerged and lost in the attempt to communicate what he sees. If he comes to feel that the vision cannot be communicated, then he is totally isolated, ghettoized indeed. But if he touches the imagination of his people, he surfaces triumphantly. His (and our) sense of balance and wholeness may be restored by the ability of the human imagination to move to the transcendent perspective of "another planet" where, as David Canaan does on his mountain, the whole in microcosm can be seen.

Klein's poet languishes at the bottom of the sea; David Canaan and the piper of Arll also found union with the world, that is, became the landscape, but at the cost of their lives. In another, less fatal sense the poet's ego is *always* extinguished (in the Keatsian sense of negative capability) in his union with the world. He lies at the bottom of the sea. But the other perspective—that of the godlike mountaineer—or, as Klein has it, the view from "another planet," remains and co-exists with the first. Insofar as the reader of Klein's work now and in future may experience this double vision of immersion and transcendence occurring at once and always, he will have in himself resurrected Klein's drowned poet.

Notes

1. Tom Marshall, ed., *A.M. Klein* (Toronto: Ryerson Press, 1970).

The Mountaineer

Earle Birney

Earle Birney, who has described mankind as "a lethal species, like a huge skin cancer around the surface of earth," is perhaps our most doom-laden and pessimistic poet of the age Klein found oppressive.[1] But it is a magnificent pessimism, a tragic vision lightened by humour, humanity, and irony. Birney finds no comfort in the Christian vision that gives joy even in the face of disaster to writers like Pratt; he seems to be a natural stoic. Probably he learned much from and was encouraged by his older friend Pratt, just as Pratt was encouraged by Roberts in the 1920's, Al Purdy by Birney more recently, and numbers of younger poets by Al Purdy, but his attitudes were always different from Pratt's. Pratt is a Christian humanist, Birney a humanist. Still, he shares Pratt's fascination with biology and geology, and his vocabulary can be equally technical.

"Think no more than you must," he writes, "of the simple unhuman truth of this emptiness" ("Pacific Door"). Yet again and again his poems afford us sharp glimpses of man dwarfed and often destroyed by an unhuman emptiness. Between "Slug in Woods" and the famous "David" there is a shift in perspective that is tragic. Near the close of the latter poem the unfortunate narrator, Bobby, "squelches" a slug, and horror rises again in his nostrils as he flees from the corpse of the friend, lying "still as a broken doll," he has had to kill. In "Slug in Woods" Birney gives us a slug's-eye view, and in "David" two boys climb mountains to achieve something like a god's-eye view. The imagery suggests that they are climbing to the sun, like Icarus. So many of the poets—C.G.D. Roberts, D.C. Scott, Frank Scott on Ararat—have wanted this long, large perspective. But in "David" the god's-eye view turns out to be a slug's-eye view after all. "As flies to wanton boys are we to the gods, they kill us for their sport." In his encounter with an impossible moral dilemma the idealistic Bobby is abruptly and brutally initiated into the hard world of human responsibility and human guilt. For guilt, in some form or other, informs most of Birney's work: it seems never to be wholly exorcised. "Bushed," another famous poem, seems almost a mythic compression of "David." The protagonist has "invented a rainbow but lightning struck it," and as his paranoia deepens into bush madness, he feels that the mountain peak is an arrowhead that will pierce his heart. In "Biography" the protagonist is scarcely better off at the end with "ice knuckling his eyes."

In "David" the mountains are sometimes described in terms of water, as a "frozen ocean," which suggests that they are not solid after all but fluid and treacherous. Human and animal terms—shoulders, fist, finger, cliff-face, talon, fang, "the thirsting lichens"—convey in a somewhat subliminal way the narrator's, and the reader's, unconscious tendency to regard the mountains as living beings. This "primitive" attitude becomes explicit in the bush madness that erupts in "Bushed." There is a tendency as well to regard nature as hostile even when it is only indifferent. The sun imagery that runs through the poem suggests at first a glorious goal and destiny, but the sun becomes an enemy to those whose aspiration takes them too high, as in the case of Icarus: when the glory is gone Bobby speaks of a "sun-cankered snowbridge." Beauty turns to horror and endless guilt. The poem has only one-dimensional characterizations, but the marvellously evocative description of life in the Rockies and the symbolic resonance of the simple tale of adventure that turns to tragedy and bitter initiation make the poem an impressive performance. A short story could not have conveyed with the same rhythmic excitement this fundamental experience. It is technically more sophisticated than any narrative of Pratt's, employing flexible, sometimes run-on quatrains with a subtle but effective assonantal rhyme-scheme (ABBA). It fully deserves its status as Canadian classic; nobody—not even Ralph Gustafson—has written better about the mountains.

Other impressive early poems are "Bushed" and "Vancouver Lights." Birney is, among other things, the poet of Vancouver, that strange outpost trapped between ocean and mountains:

> On this mountain's brutish forehead with terror of
> space
> I stir   of the changeless night and the stark ranges
> of nothing   pulsing down from beyond and between
> the fragile planets   We are a spark beleaguered
> by darkness   this twinkle we make in a corner of
> emptiness
> how shall we utter our fear that the black
> Experimentress

will never in the range of her microscope find it   Our
   Phoebus
himself is a bubble that dries on Her slide   while the
   Nubian
wears for an evening's whim a necklace of nebulae.

One could hardly find a better example than these long lines from "Vancouver Lights" afford of an essential Canadian situation: the man on the mountain who sees the fragility of the little light (civilization) created in the larger darkness. Nature is "brutish"; "terror of space" in Canada leads inevitably, as in Archibald Lampman, to thoughts of cosmic void or cosmic indifference. If there are gods, Birney feels, then man may be a tiny, probably unnoticed specimen in their cosmic experiment. The Mystery is seen, interestingly enough, as female and dark: something irrational or at least unknowable. It is worth noting in passing that women and women's values play almost as minimal a role in Birney's poetry as they do in Pratt's. Both seem to be rationalists, but where Pratt's muscular Christianity affords hope, Birney's secular gaze at hard fact leads to despair. The world appears to have gotten worse, and Pratt's belief in mechanical progress seems naive in a time that sees the essential balance of the planet threatened.

Birney's very masculine habit of mind may help to explain why he is unable to accept or "swallow" the darkness as a part of himself and the world. This does not mean passive acquiescence and the end of struggle; it means the realization that man is the struggle. Both Pratt and Birney have realized this, but in their work they tend to direct their gaze steadily outwards—even if one exults while the other laments. In "The Truant" Pratt defies the enemy joyously; Birney insists gloomily in "Vancouver Lights" that man has made his own light and will probably destroy himself too. No gods or cosmic energies need, after all, apply.

The early Birney employed fairly traditional forms, though often with a technical brilliance that transformed them. He was also a very impersonal poet, again like Pratt. The Birney who emerges in the 1960's after a long silence, however, makes a more flexible use of his own speaking voice and introduces a version of himself into his poems. He is more colloquial and displays a considerable ear for the colloquial speech of others—Canadians, South Americans, Australians. He is still, much of the time, a narrative poet, but now he has created a comic persona—the aging, somewhat bemused professor-poet—to be his narrator. This engaging fellow is no more the man Birney in all his complexity than the shambling, plain-spoken Al of the poems is the whole Al Purdy, but he is a useful character, and perhaps influenced by the Purdy persona. And he is a traveller, another Canadian Odysseus. As Purdy has recently done, Birney finds new subject matter in globe-trotting, new occasions for the expression of his ironic and pessimistic vision.

In fact, early or late, Birney's typical protagonist is an explorer (sometimes a mountaineer) or traveller—Captain Cook or Byron or Hiram Bingham or, most often now, Birney himself. The traveller is searching for vision, something more than mere knowledge or ordinary insight. Birney apparently does not believe that all artists are "mystical" by instinct, whether they consciously believe in anything of the kind or not; but he does admit that when he writes he is exorcising "unpredictable emblems of the Whole" that appear to arise from the trivia of his experience in order to appease a madman inside himself.[2] He is, then, demon-haunted, perhaps even god-haunted, even if he wishes it otherwise. But "it is not easy to free/myth from reality," as he notes in "The Bear on the Delhi Road," and the poet, especially the poet who begins with fact, as Pratt, Birney, and Purdy customarily do, must search diligently in the real world for those epiphanies that allow him to release and project energies and visions buried deeply within him. In "El Greco: Espolio," for instance, Birney "finds" in the great painting two carpenters with two kinds of integrity. The first is the prophet on the cross for his "notions of preaching," and the other is the hard pragmatist who nails him to it, "working alone in that firm and profound abstraction" that "keeps the back turned from death" and reflecting, "Criminals come in all sorts...are as mad or sane as those who decide on their killings." It seems that either Christ is mad or society is mad, depending upon one's perspective, or else both are mad, that is, it is a wholly mad universe. This nihilistic view appears very tempting to Birney: perhaps this is yet another example of Canadian ambivalence. It is interesting that the poem is spoken at first by someone observing the painting but that the voice gradually becomes indistinguishable from that of the pragmatic carpenter who does not know quite what to make of Christ.

More positively, the reader is also encouraged to consider the possibility that both the moral passion and spiritual vision of the crucified man and the cool technical facility of the carpenter may be necessary to free myth (significance, community, civilization) from reality. If this suggests a spirit of involvement in mankind as well as a commitment to detached craftsmanship, then Birney has plenty of both. Art must not be detached from a sense of human concern, even though craftsmanship involves a kind of detachment. A sense of guilt both personal and cultural is no doubt reinforced by this play of demands upon the poet. In "Arrivals" Birney speaks of a dead lawyer's "longfingered hand/stretched in some arresting habit of eloquence/to the last irrational judgement/roaring in from the storm," and feels that it is now "hooked" in him "like a third": he too must question on behalf of his fellows the apparent irrationality of existence.

This compulsion seems to be an outlet for the guilt found in early poems. An impressive example is "Cartagena De Indias" in which the poet feels accused by the hostile eyes of the wretched and diseased poor of Colombia and seeks "another bridge [than a Colombian's sister for sale] from my stupid wish/to their human acceptance." In this case the "bridge" is the poet Luis Lopez and his townspeople's ironic respect for him. Here the poet is afforded a joking affection for his otherwise largely thankless role as spokesman for and critic of his wretched folk.

Birney's continuing human concern has expressed itself in other ways as well—in scathing but accomplished and delightful satires ("Anglosaxon Street," "Canada: Case History," "Ballad of Mr. Chubb") and in moving meditations on the "terror of space," on war, on the probable fate of the unregenerate and aggressive human animal. This is Birney's characteristically gloomy version of the long view. In "Looking from Oregon" and "November Walk Near False Creek Mouth" (as in "Vancouver Lights"), a solitary man broods upon human incapacity, decay, selfishness, and vulgarity in the face of impending disaster, solitary man on the furious edge of an ocean of chaos and irrational violence. In the earlier "Damnation of Vancouver," however, there is a ray of light, a note of hope that comes, interestingly enough, from one of the very few women to figure importantly in Birney's poems. Mrs. Anyone, the housewife as Everywoman, declares to Powers (the Great Panjandrum of this piece, and supposedly a representative of the future) that individual freedom of choice is renewable in each moment of living. If time will overwhelm her, she will nevertheless have her life. And she believes that "children, grown, may sing a doom awry." But this note of hope is not at all a typical one in Birney's work. It seldom if ever appears again, though there is much wit, good humour, and high spirits— often expressed in the form of concrete poems—in Birney's latest work: this is an aspect of his ample Chaucerian talent.

For the most part, Birney's attitude to God or the possibility of any ultimate meaning or pattern remains one of lonely and courageous and essentially masculine scepticism. And Birney is, by any standard, one of the best poets Canada has produced. He is a poet of fact, like Roberts and Pratt before him, or Purdy and Newlove after him, rather than a poet of dream, like Carman, Klein, P.K. Page, Layton, Cohen, Atwood, MacEwen, and others. But eventually the distinction breaks down and ceases to be useful. A poet as good as Birney expresses a great deal of his psychic life in his realistic narratives, just as a poet of dream always tells us a good deal about the world of fact. He begins with fact and proceeds to vision rather than travelling the other way, presumably because he is sceptical of the vision that wells up from within. This almost scientific empiricism, this apparent distrust of the sources of his own creativity, could undermine the poet; instead it has played its part in shaping a poetry that is tough-minded and often bleakly magnificent.

Notes

1. Al Purdy, "The Man Who Killed David," *Weekend Magazine*, 14 December 1974.
2. Preface, *Selected Poems* (Toronto: McClelland and Stewart, 1966).

The Swimmer's Moment

Irving Layton

Birney's typical man stands on a mountain where he can see the harsh truths of the world; Irving Layton's typical man is a swimmer, one who plunges into the life of elemental passions and delights in that life, even though it be tragic. Layton advocates a Dionysian engagement with immediate experience in those poems in which he immerses himself in the "cold, green element." He wrote his earliest poem of engagement and joyous initiation, "The Swimmer," in the early 1940's; it was only in the late 1950's, however, that his lack of inhibition, ribald humour, and life-affirming vitality won their public reward. He became then that unusual phenomenon —a genuinely popular poet. After years of the kind of indifference and neglect that had contributed to A.M. Klein's collapse, Layton's moment had come, presumably because his country was at last ready for such a one.

He has remained a popular poet: brilliant, prolific, uneven, pungent, and vigorous, pleasing and irritating in large proportions In puritan Canada he brought sexual frankness and a necessary dose of animal sanity into poetry at about the same time that John Diefenbaker was transforming the political scene with his magnetic, if short-lived, appeal to some sense of self that had been starved in Canadians. It might, in fact, be argued that, as changes have occurred ever more rapidly in Canada, we have continued to enjoy Layton, especially in our most immediate and most superficial response to his work, for some of the same reasons that we have continued to enjoy Mr. Diefenbaker. A blast of old-fashioned rhetorical bluster, comic exaggeration, or moral outrage now and then is extremely refreshing in the heyday of cooler, and in some respects more deadly, customers like, say, Trudeau and Atwood. Styles in poets and politicans do, sometimes, change together (does this make Purdy our Lester B. Pearson? But that way lies madness...), but former styles can still please, and in any case what haunts the imagination has to do with something deeper than the immediate satisfactions of a style.

Birney's message to Canadians is one of stoic pessimism; Layton, in contrast, offers the possibility of liberation into a larger, freer life, if only one surrenders to vital experience. He is the unlikely heir of Carman, that much more timid swimmer, as Birney is the heir of Roberts the mountaineer. But liberation is not, of course, Layton's only major theme; he has hooked the darkness too. The other side of the cosmic coin—the vision of tragedy—is one that has been increasingly stressed in his work. This goes much deeper than the particular political and sexual attitudes which it is supposed to support. It is, as in Atwood later on and in many other Canadian poets before and since, the predatory nature of the world that haunts the swimmer. Aware of death, Layton is aware of the consequent necessity of making the most of life and of art. He celebrates; he is not a victim or a prophet of doom. He knows, as his friend Leonard Cohen puts it in a poem addressed to him, "that frelilachs end," and a poem like "Vexata Quaestio" shows this, but this is courageous realism, not despair. For a man to accept his own place fully, he must accept his death. Then he is free from the fear that is a constant pressure and inhibition or, at special times, a spur to senseless violence. The fear still exists but, recognized, it may be transformed into creative energy.

"The Birth of Tragedy" is, as most critics have noted, a central poem in this regard. The title makes the influence of Nietszche explicit here, but it is evident in all of Layton's work (as is the Heraclitean outlook he shares with Purdy, Avison and a number of other Canadian poets). This is a poem about the poet's function. Like "The Cold Green Element" and "Keewaydin Poetry Festival," it can be read as a kind of footnote to Klein's "Portrait of the Poet as Landscape." In a poem, says Layton, and in the poet's sensibility (the interface, the continual commerce between inner and outer worlds), "nature's divided things" are brought together into a unified microcosm. He believes, as Klein did, that man collaborates in the continual creation of the universe. The poet is a "mouth" for the landscape. He appeals to the "perfect gods," specifically, as Layton declared once during a reading, Apollo and Dionysus, more generally the powers of the cosmos or of his own self (or both, since power is everywhere), to sustain "passionate meditations" and give sanction to the "insurgent blood" that society fears and condemns.

The poet is a paradoxical creature: a "quiet madman" lying "like a slain thing" to receive the world passively. He is at the bottom of the sea, but he will surface in the active re-creation of the vision in words. The poet's resurrection is the momentary re-creation or birth of the world in him. "Birthday candles" are therefore blown by "someone from afar off" (God, the poet's own genius, or the poet as "nth Adam"), while "living things arrange their death" as the life-cycle proceeds. Inner and outer worlds (the worlds of Layton's mystical father and his earthy mother), Apollonian ideal and Dionysian flux, male and female are held in what Layton calls "an ironic balance of tensions"; they are "preserved for a time in suspension."[1]

"The Cold Green Element" develops the same tension between life and death in surrealistic fashion, communicating its meaning by a succession of suggestive images, as certain dreams do. The "wind and its satellite," "the black-hatted undertaker," the speaker's heart beating in the grass, the dead poet hanging from the city gates, the hunchback tree that was struck by lightning, the old women in whose eyes the sun becomes a bloodsmear on catalpa leaves, the howling black dog in the blood; as in a dream, everything is the dreamer; everything here is the speaker, the poet. The world is internalized; Layton is, like Klein and those later notable swimmers, Cohen, MacEwen, and Atwood, a poet of dream. He has—in the underwater world of his deeper consciousness—*become* the landscape. The swimmer plunges into elemental passions and realities: death, self-exposure, psychic deformity at the hands of the world, age, animal terror. But a man can choose courage and celebration in the face of death:

> the furies clear a path for me to the worm
> who sang for an hour in the throat of a robin,
> and misled by the cries of young boys
>   I am again
> a breathless swimmer in that cold green element.

With the aid of the furies, who are closely related to the perfect gods of "The Birth of Tragedy," the swimmer persists while life lasts.

"Keewaydin Poetry Festival" is more obviously comparable to Klein's "Portrait" than the two poems discussed above. It offers thumbnail sketches, a kind of multiple-exposure photograph of the poet(s), as Klein does, but this time the poets are named: Smith, Scott, Dudek and Robert Currie (whom Layton obviously disliked). But the strategy of the poem is reminiscent of another notable series of portraits: those of the the Irish revolutionaries in Yeats's "Easter 1916." Just as Yeats gives the reader every possible reason to ridicule, despise and condemn these vainglorious and fanatical men before consigning them to the immortality and "terrible beauty" of legend, Layton tells us what is wrong with our poets, and poets generally, before exalting the poet's function as "mouth." This is, of course, what Klein has done too. Klein's poets are anonymous, since this is part of his major theme. Still, this anonymity is slyly breached even as it is stressed in the phrase "a Mr. Smith in a hotel register." Klein's poets are menial in society at large; they mistake technique for communication like a watch that has twenty-one jewels but does not tell the time; they turn political and become ventriloquist's dummies for politicians; they go mystical and even mad; they suffer from extreme alienation as their proper place in the eyes of the world is usurped by businessmen, politicians, scientists and pop-singers. Twenty years later, in the person of Leonard Cohen, the poet *becomes* the pop-singer or, as Klein put it, "the troubadour." In all of this Klein, who later wrote propaganda for Samuel Bronfman, attempted a political career and suffered mental breakdowns, obviously implicates himself as well as his friends. But he proceeds to an affirmation of the poet's importance and function even in a society that is indifferent.

Layton finds his poets in a natural setting where the insects at the window, "hungry, harried, hopeful,/Clamouring," and the trees competing for sustenance are analogous to their clamouring egotism. Nature is indifferent to poetry, and so is society: the poets are building "tall monuments/Of remaindered verse." Still, only man has language; only the poet can give voice to the landscape:

> though not trees
> Green and egotistical making
> Somehow a forest of peace,
> Nor a lake dropped like a stone
> Into the stillness which thereafter
> Reproves the intruder in liquid
> Accents; though no unsullen harebells
> But a congregation of sick egotists,
> We shall endure, and they with us;
> Our names told quietly across
> These waters, having fixed this moment
> In a phrase which these—trees, flowers, birds—
> For all their self-assertion cannot do.

More determined than Klein, Layton proceeds in his later work to develop a myth of the poet as conquering hero, as representative man prophesying to a sick culture (in powerful visions like "The Improved Binoculars," a condensed modernization of Lampman's "City of the End of Things," in "The Fertile Muck," "God, When You Speak," and "Me, the PM and the Stars," in which he invokes the "sage," Nietzsche), as one who prepares the way for and celebrates, if he cannot always embody, "the free individual—independent and gay."[2] A poem of the 1970's, "The Haunting," expresses this; the free individual is still a ghost of something-to-be, an "embodied absence." There is still ambivalence in Layton's expression of the "ironic balance" of psychological, sexual, aesthetic, and social tensions, but it is a creative and fruitful ambivalence, leading to new developments and growth.

Layton is best known as a love poet, a delighted observer of and actor in the comedy of sex. This has been much remarked, but it should be recalled that the versatile Layton persona plays many sexual roles in the poems, some of them self-deprecating, and is mock-heroic as often as heroic. An honest and tender and realistic poem like "Berry Picking," in which the man observes, with understanding and sympathy, a woman growing away from him and taking refuge in her separate world, should be sufficient answer to those who think Layton is an insensitive professional male chauvinist.

Layton's vision is Nietzschean and consciously anti-Christian as well as anti-Buddhist. He believes in the necessary ruthlessness of the man who wishes to realize himself, as "For Mao Tse-Tung," an important poem, makes clear. "A Tall Man Executes a Jig," in which all his major themes figure, shows this as well. It is remarkable among Layton's poems for its ambitiousness. Most are lyrics or "passionate meditations" or anecdotes or surrealist fables or tiny squibs or lover's complaints or celebrations or satirical attacks. Layton has, surprisingly enough, not attempted long poems, preferring to disperse his amazing energy and variety among seemingly innumerable shorter works, but the "Jig" is longer and has more scope than most. It is also significant that it abandons the lyric "I" to concentrate on a representative "tall man" (Layton himself is short and burly), who is a heroic or mythic figure of Man not to be confused with the Layton persona met elsewhere.

In the first stanza the tall man spreads his blanket on a field by a highway. Soon he becomes aware of insects like "jigging motes" in the sunlight. He does not know why they are there, but it is presumably the dying snake he discovers later that has attracted them. The gnats fascinate him and hold his attention for the first three stanzas. They are "nervous dots" that make him think of the closing sentences of Thucydides' history of the Peloponnesian War, which describe a worsening situation of intrigue and treachery, or of "Euclid having a savage nightmare," that is, geometrical forms appearing and then altering before one's eyes, a notion which may owe something to Klein's use of Euclid. The tall man is allowing himself to hallucinate, as Margaret Avison does with snowflakes in "Snow." In the second stanza the gnats are like "a chain played with by some playful / Unapparent hand," and this leads to the consideration of the chain of being as some of them descend

upon his sleeveless arm. The grass
Even the wildflowers became black hairs
And himself a maddened speck among them.
Still the assaults of the small flies made him
Glad at last, until he saw purest joy
In their frantic jiggings under a hair,
So changed from those in the unrestraining air.

Now the gnats are in his arm's hair, and he feels he is, similarly, "a maddened speck" among the wildflowers. It is a possibly endless chain. In stanza three the tall man, momentarily an insect, becomes a giant, virtually a god, who can resolve all contradictions. The endless struggle for life is something he finds exalting, even though life feeds on life. If he is a gnat to the universe, he is a god to the gnats. This is closely akin to the slug-man-universe chain, in which the mountain represents the universe, in Birney's early work. Layton's frequent identification with insects on the one hand and gods and giants on the other is another example of the Canadian ambivalence and shifting perspective, a result of the encounter with our open space.

The tall man's first exaltation is short-lived; the movement of the gnats begins to seem meaningless, an image (as in Lampman's poems) of the possibly meaningless motion of the stars and the brief life-cycle of creatures:

Yet jig jig jig, the haloing black jots
Meshed with the wheeling fire of the Sun:
Motion without meaning, disquietude
Without sense or purpose, ephemerides
That mottled the resting summer air till
Gusts swept them from his sight like wisps of smoke.
Yet they returned, bringing a bee who, seeing
But a tall man, left him for a marigold.

Here the tall man is cut down to size; there is a deliberate anticlimax at the close of stanza three, where the bee displays, as is his wont, more interest in a marigold.

In stanza four the tall man abandons his "aureole of gnats" and shifts his attention to the sunset, which he perceives as a dying god pierced by a mountain: all emotional experience seems to be washed into a pool of blood on the mountainside. Surely a revelation is at hand, thinks the tall man, who is inclined to thoughts on metaphysics, art, and theology; but no, there is a second anticlimax. "Some birds chirped. Nothing else." Nature appears to be indifferent to the Christian vision of sacrifice.

Then, in stanza five, the man sees one hill "raised like a hairy arm, dark/With pines and cedars against the stricken sun/—the arm of Moses or of Joshua." Joshua once stopped the sun in order to continue a battle; as long as his arm was raised, the day continued. Here, Layton seems to endorse the defiance of Jewish heroes—in this case, it is a defiance of time and death—and to reject the Christian notion of self-sacrifice. He has said that the valour and life-affirming vitality of the Hebrew prophets have had a more profound influence on him than the work of any more recent writers, and this is no doubt true. He cannot, however, deny the fact of death, as the tall man's identification with the wounded grass snake, which follows, indicates.

Letting his focus narrow from the "halo of mountains," which had succeeded the "aureole of gnats" as the range or magic circle of his meditation (that is, his extension of his own consciousness to take in the cosmos), the tall man now discovers death in an immediate form: the violated grass snake. This is said to present a "temptation": probably the temptation to "useless" pity or else to curse existence, both of which are resisted. The snake is not seen as Satan the tempter, though Layton is no doubt playing on that echo, but as a force of life as in D.H. Lawrence's poem "Snake."

Layton has written many fine poems about animals. These have been partly encouraged by the animal poems of D.H. Lawrence, an admitted influence on his work and thought. Many of his satirical poems, for instance, are obviously akin to Lawrence's *Pansies*. Like Lawrence, Layton writes of animals both as fellow creatures, unique in their own spheres of consciousness but kin to man in the great evolutionary chain of being, and as particular symbolic expressions of the life-force in everything. An interest in animals, and an identification with them, is, in any case, natural enough in Canada: Birney, Souster, Purdy and many other writers have also written sensitively about them, both as victims of human greed and rapacity and more generally as figures of our own mortality.

Layton's grass snake, one of many significant snakes in his work, is described realistically in a somewhat Lawrentian simile as lugging his "intestine like a small red valise." At the same time, he has once embodied the "mirth and arrogant green flame of life," manifesting "earth's vivid tongue that flicked in praise of earth" like Lawrence's grander Sicilian snake. But now his jig, his dance of life, is up. The flies come like kites, dancing their jig, which will, like that of the stars, cease in its turn. Knowing this, the tall man watches the snake stiffen, opening its mouth to scream a "last silent scream that shook the black sky," and then lies down beside it in "fellowship of death."

Now his mind tunnels, "with flicking tongue" like that of the snake which had praised the earth, backward along the evolutionary chain to the bleak places where animals have met their deaths. This is Layton's version of the long view, one akin to Pratt's, Birney's, and Purdy's.

> Meanwhile the green snake crept upon the sky,
> Huge, his mailed coat glittering with stars that made
> The night bright, and blowing thin wreaths of cloud
> Athwart the moon; and as the weary man
> Stood up, coiled above his head, transforming all.

Suddenly the cosmic perspective is restored. The star-snake becomes a type of the cosmic serpent who bites his own tail, a symbol of the cosmos itself, of infinity and eternity, or at very least of the continuing life-cycle. The universe itself continues. Life persists, though individual things die. The extension of consciousness involved in this apprehension—in the mind of the poet and in his art—redeems existence, "transforming" darkness into light. It is a kind of resurrection, a lesson implicitly articulated as well in Klein's "Portrait."

Because it combines so many of his concerns and expresses them so powerfully, "A Tall Man" is probably Layton's finest single poem. As usual in his best poems, recurrent images—here the halo and circle imagery (which is ambivalent or shifting in significance, as in Lampman), the imagery of blood and wounds, the dance of life and death—convey the essential meaning. The allusions to Greek, Hebrew, and other cultures act as reinforcement.

The later Layton, like the recent Purdy, has written many poems of travel: both, perhaps, were nudged by Birney toward this particular way of renewing one's imaginative powers. Birney fares best in this endeavour, though, perhaps because it was always close to his heart. With marvellous exceptions, many of Layton's and Purdy's travel poems fail to transcend reportage. Indeed, the prose journals, observations, and aphorisms in Layton's *The Whole Bloody Bird* are more interesting than the poems. As a poet he has not undergone much technical development. He was from the beginning a fine craftsman in a variety of traditional forms or derivatives thereof—the neatness and point of many of the earliest poems show this. But he has not been a technical innovator: both the bardic voice and the colloquial one have been heard before, and only the latter contributes anything to the development of a Canadian poetic idiom. As a craftsman Layton has been too traditional and eclectic and not exploratory enough. In his introduction to *The Shattered Plinths* he speaks rightly of a new situation confronting the poet in the apocalyptic twentieth century, but he fails in that book to bring to it that new and appropriate expression that would embody the Canadian or other distinctive perspective of it.

But then, who has? One asks a great deal of Layton because he has given a great deal. With Birney, Purdy, and Margaret Avison, he takes his place with ease among the best poets writing in English today anywhere. More than this, his importance to Canadians is not to be equated with his very considerable achievement as a poet, nor, incidentally, with the soundness or error of his particular political views. He has been, paradoxically, both more and less than a poet—he is a writer and a visionary.

Irving Layton fulfils his own requirements for the poet; that he reveal the horror as well as the glory of existence and also the fierce joy of living in the face of the horror. Thus one may triumph over death in the intensity and verve of one's living and in the living utterance of poetry. Layton distrusts art, perhaps because he is a natural writer to whom many things have come spontaneously. In "The Graveyard" he writes that art stills the contraries— but it may be the stillness of death. Perhaps this is why he has not pursued further a formal exploration: he might lose the moment. Perhaps, however, there is another, a further art, if we can find and thus create it, one that is in Layton's own words "Forever dislodging / the framework for / its own apprehension" ("Enemies").

Notes

1. "Introduction," *A Red Carpet For The Sun* (Toronto: McClelland and Stewart, 1959).
2. Ibid.

War Poets and Postwar Poets

The other notable poets of Irving Layton's generation have received less attention from the general public than he has, but they have shared in the general broadening of sensibility and refinement of technical resources that occurred in the 1940's and 1950's. Even the most "timeless" art is created at a particular moment of time, and it worth noting that Layton emerged from the second "Montreal group" of the 1940's, the second wave of poetic activity in that city. With Louis Dudek and that potentially great critic and editor, John Sutherland (then his brother-in-law), he was actively involved in *First Statement* and certainly aware of the rival magazine *Preview*. *Preview* featured the veterans Scott, Smith, and Klein, but it also included such newcomers as P.K. Page and the English writer Patrick Anderson, who was an important catalyst for some of the others. At this time Layton saw Klein regularly, and they talked about poetry. *First Statement* gave us work by Layton, Dudek, Raymond Souster and Miriam Waddington. At the same time Alan Crawley's fine magazine *Contemporary Verse* presented a wider spectrum of poets—including Anne Marriott, Birney, and Livesay —from its home base in Vancouver.[1] Still other poets—Douglas LePan, Wilfred Watson, George Johnston, Eldon Grier, R.A.D. Ford—emerged in the period without significant association with any new magazine.

Patrick Anderson's early poems have not worn well. Apparently intoxicated by the style of Dylan Thomas, this visiting Englishman was moved to pen windily rhetorical rhapsodies that do not bear too much examination, since they have so little real content. Consequently, his remarkable verbal and metaphorical facility is more wearying than sustaining: Auden and Thomas have overwhelmed what might be genuine Anderson. But Anderson stimulated Page, and probably Klein (who did have something to say), and he has, more recently, written good poems set in his native countryside. Unfortunately, his ambitious "Poem on Canada," which contains some highly evocative passages, has to be called a noble failure, basically something willed, faked; but it may well have influenced later, more deeply knowledgeable Canadian poets to attempt their own versions of the poem that is Canada.

The *Preview* poets show mainly British influences, the *First Statement* poets, with the significant exception of the eclectic Layton, predominantly American influences. This seems almost too neat a Canadian division, a compromise of colonialisms, but the *First Statement* poets, at least those consciously North American ones like Dudek and Souster, do look forward to the development of a Canadian voice and idiom that comes with Purdy, whose first really distinctive work they published at their Contact Press in the 1960's.

Dudek's early poems of an imagist clarity, influenced by William Carlos Williams and the young Pound, are a refreshing alternative to the pyrotechnics of Anderson, but a little of this kind of innocent observation goes a long way. Apparently he was conscious of this himself, since he turned to metaphysical observations about the acts of perception and creation and to long meditative sequences such as *Europe, En México*, and *Atlantis*. These are his equivalents of Pratt's long narratives; he has learned from Pound that a long poem now has to be some sort of musical sequence. Unfortunately, much of the observation in *Europe* seems commonplace— little more than a tourist's jottings. Yet there are splendid passages too, and a clean, straightforward style of utterance, a Greek clarity, that wears infinitely better than the extremes of metaphorical density favoured by the English-oriented poets. And *En México*, more powerful and more concentrated, is highly successful, however much Whitmanesque "all is good" it utters. Like *Europe, Atlantis* is too long, but it has magnificent passages. Dudek ponders men and plants and animals as they reveal the twin reality of good and evil, the double hook, and wonders if evolution itself is "a growing up," since pity seems to be "a recent idea of God's." This is akin to Jung's view and to those hints of it detected in Pratt.

> Can we imagine the adulthood of us all?
> The gods within us, aching to be real.

Here, as in all of Dudek's meditations, is the Canadian habit of taking the long view of evolution. This places him in an honourable tradition involving D.C. Scott, E.J. Pratt, F.R. Scott, Earle Birney, A.M. Klein, Irving Layton, Al Purdy, and Margaret Avison (not to mention such novelists as Grove, MacLennan and Laurence), all of whom wrestle with time and space and the god or gods of evolution. Dudek's career has been a striving after a flexible open form that can contain his observation-meditation. In this he is close to Avison and Purdy. And his later poems become more and more impressive as the reader surrenders to them. When he writes of the Rockies Dudek touches—perhaps deliberately—on that sense of the Good which George Grant (in *Technology and Empire*) has declared that we have lost:

> Evenings, the deckle-edged hills help us:
> certainly as something good, that speaks for itself.

> And in the morning
> the wave-movement of the hills
>   like that wave-theory of matter
> where fruit-trees flower in their folds
> as the right wave-lengths gather in the Good.

> I have believed that the whole universe is speech, a
>   communication.
> That speaks for itself. And wants to be believed to be
>   seen.
>   "A Circle Tour of the Rockies"

Dudek is the poet-as-thinker. Miriam Waddington, by contrast, has a rare and fine lyric gift that puts her in the poetic company of such as Bliss Carman and Leonard Cohen; but she attempted to be a realistic poet too. On the whole, it is the poems of love and loss, of memory and vision intermingled, rather than the poems of social work and, more recently, of Canada, commendable though these are, that are most appealing: poems like "Interval," "Catalpa Tree," "In the Sun," "The Season's Lovers," "Goodby Song," "Icons," and "The Bright Room." Like Dudek, Waddington has improved with time; her best poems are characterized by delicacy and precision and passionate honesty (though this has its limits). She has advanced as a craftsman to a near perfect control of her particular medium. She has always had a feeling for natural things and for landscape. Recently, this has been extended in engaging poems about Canadians, Canada, and the poet's attachment to them, but these lack the intensity and depth that characterizes the nostalgic love poems and poems about family. In these she is a more surrealistic Dorothy Livesay, telling of her life, its successes and failures. It is a poetry of haunting moments and at its best it haunts the reader. Waddington's private world is the green world of past experience as it lives on in the soul. She sings the autonomy of the human imagination in an increasingly perilous and unobliging world. She is a survivor, not an explorer, and her weapons are wit and courage. Often she attempts to "draw wit for a wire/around situations" ("Incidents for the Undying World"). Underlying the recurrent themes of lost love, encroaching age and the sacred tie of blood is an insistence on the primary reality of the world of vision that enables her to declare jubilantly or defiantly: "My old age/is dancing" ("New Year's Day"). Taken altogether, the poems constitute not only a lament for lost happiness but a joyful affirmation of ultimate purity.

But this Blakean "innocence" is her limitation as well as her strength. It gives an extra dimension to her work, but there is no breakthrough into a further realm of richer understanding, only an honest confession of bewilderment. The protagonist of these intensely personal poems is unable to comprehend evil or malice, in others or in herself:

> the other
> things that harmed her
> (even herself), those
> she could never explain

"Things of the World"

In her *A.M. Klein*, Miriam Waddington has written that there is no Jewish concept of "original sin." Human aggression is perhaps inexplicable to the Calvinist too, as Hugh MacLennan's novels would seem to suggest. In any case, Waddington refuses to surrender an ideal image of herself and the world. Therefore, despite her experience of social work, she cannot effectively explore the reality of evil, as Layton, another consciously Jewish poet of dream, has done. Her poems are nevertheless the impressive product of an unvanquished inner integrity:

> Closed in this small tight room
> there is a warm illimitable
> thing inside me keeps me
> alive and proud and sane.

"Second Generation"

Raymond Souster is probably Canada's most successful imagist, the equivalent of William Carlos Williams. The American influence is obvious, but Souster has been highly successful in creating a poetic universe that is both objective in its detailed observation and yet uniquely and unmistakeably his own. This universe is, for the most part, the city of Toronto as it is known to a particular sensibility. In this respect, as in his concern for "little" people, Souster is something of a poetic Morley Callaghan. He is obsessed, not only with the small joys of urban existence but with the lot of the outcast and lonely: people, animals, and objects (especially damaged objects) become images of some deep, ultimate loneliness and sense of death in the poet himself. Souster's subject matter is in fact reasonably varied, but the obsessive way in which he returns to winos, strippers, prostitutes, cripples and wounded animals in poems representing thirty years of work can give an impression of limited range. But he is more than an honest chronicler: he develops a myth of the fragility and stubborn determination of living things in a cold, uncaring world. The refuge of men and other animals is a recurring theme. The hibernating groundhog turns up in a number of poems (including "The Hunter," which is justly celebrated by critics); man's own refuge is in dream, in poetry, in sexual love.

That Souster's whole work is more impressive than most of its individual parts seems undeniable. In his case there are no major or especially ambitious poems like "A Tall Man Executes A Jig" or "David." Taken from the context of the whole body of work, a Souster poem may strike one as slight or formless or prosy or sentimental. Or it may be a significant moment perfectly caught, expressed so directly and exactly that the poem is translucent.

Souster's participation in the Second World War—dealt with in his novel *On Target*—is the source of a few very impressive poems that go far away from his usual urban Canadian world. It is the larger context and the sense of man's bewilderment in a vast world of pain and confusion that makes these poems especially appealing. There is a sense of modern man at large in a world he cannot understand, a world out of control. It is a world that reveals in stark form man's inconsistencies:

> Caught in the cone of searchlights over Hamburg
> he prayed: Lord, get me out
> and I'll make it up to You....
>
> So the next evening
> got stoned in the mess, laid a crying
> sixteen-year old up a Darlington lane.

> "World Traveller at Twenty-One"

Here Souster has a larger backdrop, or "objective correlative" even—the confusion and drama of the war—for his vision of man's inescapable fragility and loneliness. The war brought out the best in him.

The war wrung lines from other Canadians: Bertram Warr (who died too soon for us to know what he might have done), George Whalley, Douglas LePan. These were men of no special connection with movements or magazines or poetry "scenes." Yet George Whalley's poems have a hard imagist clarity that is as striking as Souster's; LePan's style, in contrast, is richer and more rhetorical, like that of Klein, Hart Crane, or Dylan Thomas (and behind them the great Elizabethans, perhaps especially Spenser).

Whalley is especially good at capturing movement and atmosphere:

> The long Northern nights. Cold alone
> heartsick miserable, you speak to a lookout
> and it isn't your voice that speaks. A book in your bunk
> after the watch is over; but still you listen
> sensitively alive, even in sleeping,
> to every change in speed course sound.
> Today we had a *bath*. Of course I was last
> but God it was good, the hot water and the soap.
>
> "Seascape 1940-1941"

The tone is rather more tight-lipped, but it is easy to imagine Souster writing this.

Douglas LePan writes too of the experience and the effect of war in his second collection of poems, *The Net and the Sword*, but in a much more highly charged language:

> A peacock train of stars along the water-stairs
> Of the castled hill;
> And the mild eye, innocent of its destiny,
> Now lips the lymph and milky dream of heaven...
>
> Then systole of sky. Stillness become
> A lion's den.
> Wild meteors falling in our laps. Flames.
> Dragonish flames and cries that call for breath.
> The sphinctered sky seals off a livid bell-jar
> On humiliated animals lost in holes.
>
> "An Effect of Illumination"

Beauty is blasted by the shock of bombardment. The poet achieves a resonance, an intimation of other wars and older civilizations in travail, with this heightened language, a language that seems appropriate to the historic Italian scenes his regiment of soldiers passes through. LePan has also written important poems on Canada, notably "A Country Without a Mythology" and "A Rough, Sweet Land," which are much more telling in their expression of the experience of transplanted European man in the new world than those of Patrick Anderson. But it is these war poems, his meditations on "a species preying on itself" and on the nature of simple animal heroism through the ages, that win for him a unique place among Canadian poets. Most of the important ones have pondered the meaning of evolution and man's apparent perversity, and some—Pratt and Birney, for instance—have written of the war, but LePan's treatment of the actual experience of combat gives *The Net and the Sword* some of the power of a prose work like *The Red Badge of Courage*. It seems that LePan is attempting to exorcise intense memories and deeply personal emotions. His book can usefully be set beside Colin McDougall's superb novel, *Execution*, which also deals with the Italian experience of Canadians. There is doubt, fear and anguish as well as admiration for the heroic. The horror is sometimes expressed with a straightforward realism that looks forward to the powerful vision of LePan's own novel *The Deserter*:

> Guards of the house:
> A dead horse with turds half-bulging from its rump,
> A sergeant dead in the ditch, half-buried,
> Green as his tunic. Verdigris blots him.
> The whites of his eyes are scrawled with flies,
> The hair of his head now dead and excremental.

> "Elegy in the Romagna"

The poet, who views desolation with a clear eye, feels like "the impotent god of a lost creation"; consciousness is " a temple where the divinity is dying." But in this situation of destitution human "pity and concern" may flower.

The war's grim truth was an occasion for high achievement to a few Canadian poets. Their work may remind one as well of the cost of John McCrae's one perfect lyric, "In Flanders Fields," in the earlier war. But there are other notable poets of this generation—Wilfred Watson (with his marvellous poem on Emily Carr), Kay Smith, Eldon Grier, George Woodcock, Anne Wilkinson, George Johnston—whose wars are elsewhere. Woodcock, Wilkinson, and Johnston, in particular, represent the growing assurance, maturity, and sophistication (an extension of the "new" poetry of Smith, Scott and Co.) that belongs to this time.

George Woodcock's early poems, written in England, are shapely in design, employing stanzas like those of Auden and Spender, and apocalyptic or doom-laden in tone like those of Dylan Thomas or those of D.H. Lawrence some twenty years earlier. The grand drama of the 1940's is placed in the larger context of the possible exhaustion of the species, yet there is hope for the new dawn that might follow the ruin. After the war the poet in Woodcock fell silent for many years, but in recent times a new flowering has occurred. The new poems are free in form and conversational in manner, more straightforward meditations on love, politics and death. Though not part of the Canadian mainstream, Woodcock's poems are a distinctive and distinguished part of his remarkably varied oeuvre.

Anne Wilkinson is a war poet in the sense that is presumably intended by J.D. Salinger when in *The Catcher in the Rye* he pronounces Emily Dickinson a better war poet that Rupert Brooke. It makes sense to think of Wilkinson as being at least akin to Dickinson in her expression of internal conflicts. In the United States the wry, laconic, tense self-exposition of Dickinson leads to the suicidal extremism and gallows humour of Sylvia Plath, that much-touted, smaller, latter-day Dickinson. In Canada it leads to the toughness and honesty of Dorothy Livesay and Anne Wilkinson. Incidentally, whose who think that Canadian poets are morbid and defeatist to an extreme degree will presumably have to account for the fact that their suicide rate cannot begin to compare with that of American poets: a few early deaths and some madness are about the worst that can be managed. Wilkinson was a swimmer: diving and swimming poems are frequent, and there is an elegy for drowned Virginia Woolf. Like P.K. Page and Miriam Waddington, she was influenced by nursery rhymes as well as by Dylan Thomas. Her style is direct and spare, never lush. She writes of evolution, the loss of innocence, the decay of love, and the coming of death as they do. It is a great pity that she did not live longer: the body of work she left is a distinguished one.

George Johnston is another war poet in the Dickinsonian sense. He is also the most accomplished writer of light verse (often with sombre undertones) that Canada has ever known.

> There are seventy times seven kinds of loving
>   None quite right:
> One is of making, one of arguing,
>   One of wheedling in the night
> And all the others one can think of, none quite right.
>
>   .   .   .   .
>
> They are all hard,
>   All seventy times seven, hard as can be:
> Veterans of loving are wary-eyed and scarred
>   And they can see into everything they see.

"Veterans"

In its wry wit and underlying wisdom this piece is typical of Johnston's light touch. His readers have delighted in his gallery of comic characters and his delineation of comic situations. He could even be called a Canadian Betjeman, but this would do an injustice to a distinctively Canadian consciousness and sensibility. Though he speaks in "Love of the City" of his Ottawa as "this great roof of pity," he writes also:

> I have another address
> That only I know about, out in the country,
> An island with a cave, burnt-out fires and bones.
>
> "Pied A Terre"

Johnston knows that beauty is painful because it touches on love and death. He knows as well that all men are veterans now, bumbling along as they must in a perpetual postwar world:

> Every November eleventh after the leaves have gone,
> After the heat of summer when the heats of winter come
> on,
> Ghosts from all over the country drift to the capital then
> To see what we do to remember, we left-over Ottawa
> men.
>   .   .   .   .
> Blowing our bugles and noses and making ourselves feel
> brave,
> And not only brave but prudent, and not only prudent
> but wise.
> Go to sleep ghosts, we say, and wave our wise good-
> byes.
>
> "Remembrance"

This poem is funny and sad and perhaps a bit shamefaced, a typically Canadian antidote to the genuine Canadian heroism celebrated by LePan. Perhaps it was the spirit of Leacock that came to George Johnston in Confederation Square.

Collectively, these poets represent high accomplishment and remarkable variety. Their eclecticism and formal sophistication are evidence that modernist idioms had by the 1950's been thoroughly acclimatized in Canada. It remained for others to get through and beyond eclecticism to create a distinctively Canadian poetic idiom.

Notes

1. Joan McCullagh's *Alan Crawley and "Contemporary Verse"* (Vancouver: University of British Columbia Press, 1976) deals with this otherwise mostly forgotten achievement.

PART THREE

Perspective: The Inheritors

Space and Ancestors

Al Purdy

As far as I'm concerned, I found *a* voice (not necessarily a consistent one), but I thought that I was at my best beginning about 1961-62, when *Poems for all the Annettes* was first published; I was sure I had hit a vein in which I could say many more things. I'd been looking for ways and means of doing it; and finally, it got to the point that I didn't care what I said—I'd say anything—as long as it worked for me.

Al Purdy[1]

In Al Purdy something of the spirit of Margaret Laurence's Bram Shipley of *The Stone Angel* lives again: down to earth, melancholy and ribald by turns, rambling, life-loving, pleasantly disreputable. Purdy has discovered both voice and voices: a recognizable Ontario voice and a sense of the many Canadian voices both past and present. Though he began, extraordinarily enough, as a blatant imitator of Bliss Carman in the 1940's, that enchanted echo soon palled, and after a bout of Dylan Thomas and then Irving Layton, he began at last to structure the poem to his own way of speaking. No doubt this development owed something to the example of the American "Beats" and their ancestor, Whitman, but Canadian voices are essentially different, as Purdy well knows. Since 1962 or so he has evolved a flexible free-verse idiom all his own, a kind of run-on poem in which the Heraclitean flux and flow of Canadian space is embodied as rhythm; he does not *list* things, as the Beats tended to do; there is greater flow, swifter enjambment:

Riding the boxcars out of Winnipeg in a
morning after rain so close to
the violent sway of fields it's

like running and running
naked with summer in your mouth.

"Transient"

Purdy's utterance is dominated by the present particple, the present tense.
Everything is happening now in the continuity of consciousness.

Purdy's mature poems fuse the romantic and the commonplace, as in the
description of "golden oranges of dung" in "The Cariboo Horses," and
often conclude by refusing to conclude—with a dash or some. . . . There is a
deliberate letdown or anticlimax; all goes on, continues endlessly. Dashes
and long digressions and present participles and images that unfold
endlessly into other images (here perhaps Thomas and Layton may have left
their mark) abound in a freewheeling movement, a more or less free
association of whatever pops into the poet's head. This poet dislikes the
static and embraces happily the Canadian amorphousness when he says:
"being anything was never quite what I intended" ("Song of the
Impermanent Husband"). He will not be pinned down, and can thus
remain himself—his whole self, a thing finally indefinable. He has
transcended the famous problem of identity, then, by accepting the world as
it is and himself as he is.

The invention of the Purdy line, either as long or as short as suits his
immediate purpose, and of the run-on Purdy poem, gives Al a claim to the
title of the first truly native poet. Dennis Lee has asserted[2] that Purdy is the
first poet fully to embody in his language the gestures of being here,
Canadians' perplexed refusal to be American without knowing what they
are to be, their ambivalence. It can indeed be argued that Purdy achieves in
his very uncertainty of tone, his sudden shifts of emphasis and perspective,
what A.M. Klein's eclecticism of traditional styles and rhetorics only
approximates: a genuine multiplicity of view that is appropriate to the
Canadian situation. He gets the voices right, needing no immediate aid
from the mighty dead of England, those Spensers and Shakespeares and
Miltons that Pratt and Klein evoked. Lee writes eloquently as well of
Purdy's evocation of space-time without, as Robin Mathews notes,
observing that D.C. Scott, E.J. Pratt, and Earle Birney, among others, had
taken a very long view too: "the times he has found authentic—U.E.L.
time, as it drifts like wispy snake-fences into the ground of the present, the
enduring time of prehistoric artisans: the personal time of his own loves and
hates, his parents' and grandparents'—are tenuous moments in a field that
loops back to Stone Age man and out through intergalactic light years."
Margaret Avison offers a similar span of consciousness (as well as a similar
Heraclitean sense of everything in flux). And Birney's best poems had

displayed a sense of the vast stretches of evolutionary, geological and cosmic time within which man's puny and potentially self-destructive civilization has arisen. This is something encouraged by encountering the Canadian space, as novelists F.P. Grove, Sinclair Ross, and Hugh MacLennan have also pointed out. It is not Purdy's insight alone. Nevertheless, Dennis Lee's contention is basically correct. Purdy is the first poet to embody both Canadians' sense of themselves groping in space and their confused questing for a mode of existence different from both the European and the American *in a wholly appropriate poetic form*—though it is not necessarily the only one. For this reason, all younger poets who grasp some of the meaning of his achievement are in his debt.

Like Margaret Laurence, Purdy is interested in ancestors—real ones, local ones—and in lost or disappearing cultures and peoples, some of them native peoples who may prove to be spiritual ancestors. He is also, like Pratt and Birney and Layton, possessed of a sense of man's kinship with plants and animals. He articulates both isolation and connectedness. Ancestral voices both human and natural are heard; a multiple perspective is achieved.

There is a relatively simple shift of perspective in "Trees at the Arctic Circle," one of those poems that provide an easy entry to Purdy's world. The poet at first scorns the dwarf trees of Baffin Island for their lack of heroic stature, but then he begins to see the marvel of their persistence at all in a soil that becomes permafrost two feet down. The trees become an image of Canadians' own persistence and survival in a difficult place. But Purdy does not make this significant connection explicit: it is not necessary. And in "Detail" he refuses to make a parable of the small apples that cling in "hurricane winds" like small bells—"they were there and that's all"—but the image haunts him. He may have been thinking of the apples which Layton promises to make significant in "The Fertile Muck" when he refuses to do likewise just as when he writes of frogs in an early version of "At Roblin Lake," he makes an oblique reference to the air-rifle that figures in Layton's "Cain," thus defining himself against another important poet. Purdy knows that the apples have significance whether the poet writes of them or not.

"Interruption" is a more subtle poem. In it Purdy explores the way in which man—here a man who has built a house—"interrupts" the normal flow of natural life. Human beings, he observes, set traps and must remember to avoid them themselves. It is inevitable that man will disrupt the natural world and Purdy is not sentimental about it, but at the same time he is aware of the interpenetration of animal and human worlds. As man invades nature, nature invades man's consciousness:

> Moonlight in the living room,
> a row of mice single file
> route march across the empty lunar plain
> until they touch one of my thoughts
> and jump back frightened,
> but I don't wake up.
> Pike in the lake pass and re-pass the windows
> with clouds in their mouth.

Here can be sensed, as in Margaret Avison's work, the continuity of inner and outer worlds. As in all Purdy's poems, the floating consciousness of the poet is itself both medium and message: the reader stands at the interface. Purdy perceives that animals and men are equals in the face of mortality, of extinction of consciousness.

A striking example of Purdy's feeling for other forms of life, as well as his awareness of how the world lives within man and he in it, and his ability to evoke distant ancestral voices is "In the Caves," in which an Indian who is a poor hunter, and thus for all practical purposes "useless," is haunted by the scream of a mammoth slain by his people and then driven to paint the mammoth and his scream on cave walls. This original artist, an Edvard Munch in embryo, tells his own story in familiar Purdyesque uncertain stages but without the Purdy humour, which would be as out of place here as in "The Runners," another re-creation of distant voices, and the effect is moving. Part of the effect comes from the feeling that there is an element of autobiography in this portrait of the man whose intense sensitivity helps to carry the consciousness of the race forward:

> there is something here I must follow
> into myself to find
> outside myself in the mammoth
> beyond the scorn of my people
> who are still my people
> my own pain and theirs
> joining the shriek that does not end
> that is inside me now.

In "The Beavers of Renfrew" Purdy pursues another aspect of man's place in the world when he asks:

> I wonder what screwed-up philosophy,
> what claim to a god's indulgence,
> made men decide their own importance?

and then proceeds to develop a comic myth along Indian lines in which Beaver took pity on man and guided him to a higher intelligence until man forgot the secret of the beavers—"the secret of staying completely still." The folly of human ambition, drive, aggression is suggested. Why not just stay here, the poet asks, instead of going forward to the planets?

And yet Purdy's head is in the planets a good deal of the time; the stars and moon have a habit of invading his bedroom and participating in his nocturnal activities. His personal poems with their cosmic-domestic ironic context have a range of moods from the simply tender to the mocking or burlesque to the ironic affirmative. He can identify with the feminine even while rejecting sentimentality and suspecting absolute statements, as in "Necropsy of Love." "Love is ambivalence and sex is a bully," he remarks flatly in "Love Song," and other human beings remain mysterious and wonderful and finally unknowable. Perhaps the definitive Purdy love poem is "Necropsy of Love":

> No I do not love you
> hate the word,
> that private tyranny inside a public sound,
> your freedom's yours and not my own,
> but hold my separate madness like a sword,
> and plunge it in your body all night long.
>
> If death shall strip our bones of all but bones,
> Then here's the flesh and flesh that's drunken-sweet
> as wine cups in deceptive lunar light:
> reach up your hand and turn the moonlight off,
> and maybe it was never there at all,
> so never promise anything to me:
> but reach across the darkness with your hand,
> reach across the distance of tonight,
> and touch the moving moment once again
> before you fall asleep—

All that can be known is the moving moment; nothing else is guaranteed, and only death can certify that there really was that other absolute, love. It is interesting that this poem moves from half-rhymes (word-sword, own-long) and irregular blank verse lines to the final half-line ending abruptly in a dash. Purdy moves in and out of metrical verse here as it suits his purpose, mocking the traditional love song even as he produces a new version of it.

Beyond the personal Purdy searches for connection with his own place in the long poem "In Search of Owen Roblin" and in such poems as "My

Grandfather Talking,'' ''Wilderness Gothic,'' and ''The Country North of Belleville.'' This last poem concerns the stone ''country of our defeat'' where farms have been abandoned, and already, or still, men are strangers: evocative depiction of place and oblique reference to the myths of Sysiphus and Atlantis give the poem a haunting power. ''Wilderness Gothic'' deals with the somewhat more successful, if uncongenial, pioneers of nineteeenth-century Ameliasburgh. A man sheathing the church spire, which stands up directly across Roblin Lake from the poet's dock, with new metal arouses the poet's thoughts about the passing of an age of faith. It is an autumn day on which the process of life and death continues, and human progress, that ''interruption'' of the natural, is signalled by the disappearance of the bodies of three young birds in the sub-surface of the new county highway. But the present picture is incomplete, Purdy contends, without a sense of the continuing presence of the ''gothic ancestors'' who ''peer from medieval sky,'' those faces escaped from photograph albums. Like Roch Carrier, in his comic trilogy about changing Quebec, Purdy sees the Canadian past as ''medieval,'' and it seems as if the fierce religion of the Victorians combined with the wilderness makes for a ''gothic'' world indeed. The Ontario Irish world of James Reaney's magnificent trilogy of plays, *The Donnellys,* is another example—as medieval as Ireland itself still, sometimes, seems to be. It could be argued as well, if it is not too fanciful, that settled Canada remained ''Victorian'' in its attitudes until at least 1945 and that the Renaissance has only caught up with Canadians since then. This is the necessary background to today: the scene before Purdy's eyes takes on a slightly sinister cast as he suggests sardonically that the workman on the church steeple—seen briefly as an image of man's faith in some divine purpose—may fall. Medieval superstition seems appropriate to this place: the eeriness felt by Canada's earliest poets is sounded again in Purdy's uniquely sardonic tones.

It is found as well in ''The Runners,'' Purdy's extraordinary mythic recreation of a first encounter with Canada:

> I am afraid of this dark land,
> ground mist that makes us half ghosts,
> and another silence inside silence...
> If we join our thoughts to the silence,
> if our trails join the animal trails,
> and the sun remembers what the moon forgets...
> Brother, it comes to me now,
> the long ship must sail without us,
> we stay here—

The phrase "silence inside silence" echoes very similar phrases of Duncan Campbell Scott, though possibly Purdy did not know this.

There is eeriness here. And yet, there is no sense of despair in Purdy's examination of ancestors and lost cultures. Rather, something continues eternally, exists still in the light from a distant star and in ongoing human consciousness. Continuity, communion, and community are Purdy's major themes, not victimization and defeat. "Knossos did burn," he says in "On the Decipherment of Linear B," and then he vividly re-creates the event in terms of human suffering. But it also "signalled the stars" and came to life again in the work of the unheroic professors and code-breakers. The Dorsets, he likes to think, left behind them an "ivory thought" that is "still warm" ("Lament for the Dorsets"). The past may continue into the present in the form of art or document or human fellow-feeling:

> I come here as part of the process
> in the pale morning light,
> thinking what has been thought by no one
> for years of their absence,
> in some way continuing them—
> And I observe the children's shadows
> running in this green light from
> > a distant star
> into the near forest—
> wood violets and trilliums of
> a hundred years ago
> blooming and vanishing—
> the villages of the brown people
> toppling and returning—
> What moves and lives
> > occupying the same space,
> what touches what touched them
> > owes them.

In some way the dead are continued in the consciousness of the future. The idea is beautifully stated here in "Remains of an Indian Village," one of Purdy's finest poems.

The idea involves some eternity of consciousness that exists perhaps not only in the mind but within the endless flux itself, "the moving moment," "the seasonal cycle and the planet's rhythm." Perhaps this repeated notion of continued existence owes something to the ever more extraordinary intimations of recent subatomic physics which suggest that no energy, no

event, is ever wholly lost. Or else it is simply intuitive, Purdy's version of
faith. It is a religious idea; like A.M. Klein, Purdy seems to have found a
transcendent perspective on things—"another planet" or, in his case, the
notion of all things continuing in space-time ("this green light from a
distant star").

In "Archaeology of Snow" Purdy remarks on the persistence of human
beings, and in "Method for Calling Up Ghosts," he notes

> how everything we do or say has an effect somewhere,
> passes outward from itself in widening circles,
> a sort of human magic by which
> a word moves outside the nature of a word
> as side effect of itself
>   the nature of a word being
> that when it's been said it will always be said
> —a recording exists in the main deep of sound.

Everything persists then, in human consciousness or "magic" and perhaps
also in the larger consciousness of the evolving universe, which is surely the
"main deep" of everything, if there is such a thing. John Newlove, one of
Purdy's obvious successors, has even suggested, in his long-ish poem "The
Pride," that living Canadians *become* Indians as they breathe in the dust of
their past. Purdy does not go so far as this in his poetic resurrection of the
past; he remains tentative in his expression of the possible meaning of his
intimations of immortality.

Still, the insight persists and is to be found in his most moving poems, in
the beautiful "Horseman of Agawa," for instance:

> I think that after the Ojibway are all dead
> and all the bombs in the white world have fizzed into
>   harmlessness
> the ghost of one inept hunter who always got lost
> and separated from his friends because he had a lousy
>   sense of direction
> that man can come here to get his bearings calling out
> to his horse his dog or himself because he's alone
> in the fog in the night in the rain in his mind and say
> "My friends where are you?"
> and the rock walls will seize his voice
> and break it into a million amplified pieces of echoes
> that will find the ghosts of his friends in the tombs of
>   their dust.

But Purdy no sooner indulges in this (again fairly typical) speculation about continuance and permanence than he suspects it: "I mistrust the mind-quality that tempts me / to embroider and exaggerate things." He will not be pinned down here either, even if his poems return again and again to the matter of some species of immortality. In the latter part of "The Horseman of Agawa," he observes that his wife receives the message of the rock paintings directly, while he embroiders with words. The poem is, among other things, a tribute to the immediate, silent connection of woman and Indian paintings. This female receptivity is primary, words only a pale echo of it. Purdy appreciates both male and female qualities, and thus he achieves a more whole and balanced vision of things than Pratt or Birney, those earlier poets of fact and history.

Purdy is, it seems, the national poet that Pratt set out to be, not because he has travelled all over Canada and then written it up, a procedure that sometimes induces tedium, but because he has given us the voices of the past, the ghosts, as well as those of the present. It was this immediacy that was needed, not pseudo-epic (even that informed by the verve and energy of Pratt).

There are aspects of Purdy that have been neglected here—his rollicking humour (some of it the humour of ambivalence and the sudden shift of perspective, as in Stephen Leacock); his wide learning, especially in history, anthropology, archaeology, and related fields; the metaphysical bent that sends him travelling in time and space, to large and small, in and out of Canada, but always with Roblin Lake as the omphalos, the centre of his universe; his sometimes unusual and certainly large vocabulary, which seems comparable to Pratt's, Klein's or Layton's; his marvellous conceits and subtle images ("the charging cotyledons of spring," "the trembling voltage of summer," "their seed-pods glow / like delicate grey earrings / their leaves are veined and intricate / like tiny parkas"); his social concern and his status along with Milton Acorn as a working class poet—but all of these are further evidence of his myriad-mindedness. A Purdy poem may sometimes disintegrate under the strain of his polymath rambling, but most do not. His humour and his rapid shifts of tone and subject and perspective save him from sentimentality and the falsity of making too definitive a statement about the complex, elusive, multidimensional, shifting world. "I can be two men if I have to," he says in "Love Song." In speaking for Everyman as Canadian he wants to speak for the plain man as well as the learned man, since he is both, and to articulate the uncertainty and ambivalence of the national character. He wants to present a vision that is "comic" in the largest sense, since it expresses great faith in life and the continuance of life. As in Margaret Laurence's novels about past and present, the attempt, which is "kind of ludicrous or kind of beautiful I guess" ("The Horseman of Agawa"), often succeeds magnificently.

Notes

1. Interview with Gary Geddes, in *Twentieth Century Poetry and Poetics* (Toronto: Oxford University Press 1969), p. 530.
2. *Saturday Night*, July/September 1972.

Perspective

Margaret Avison

Perspective, open space and interiors, the dual psychic rhythm of expansion and contraction, of faring forth and hibernating: all of these Canadian obsessions are found again in the brilliant, intricate and difficult work of Margaret Avison. She is a poet of the air, of open space, of the speculative soul that travels from the eye. She is a traveller, like Birney but on something akin to an astral plane.

Two poems that provide a relatively easy access to Avison's difficult journey—"The Valiant Vacationist" and "The Swimmer's Moment"— have some sense in them of acquaintance with the Niagara area. It is there that the real whirlpool and the real Brock's Monument are. But if these real places helped to shape the poems, it is of no special importance in the poems themselves.

The speaker in "The Valiant Vacationist" is climbing stone steps like those of Brock's Monument. Once this journey is begun, there is apparently no going back. Ordinary details fall away, and the extraordinary nature of things is perceived. On a "half-way landing" the vacationist encounters a fly and wants to shake his hand as "my last countryman": a curious perspective is achieved in this apparent echo of Emily Dickinson's famous imagined encounter with a fly at the moment of death. The vacationist then proceeds into a visionary kingdom of apparently symbolic landscapes something like those of Eliot's "Journey of the Magi," a likely influence on this poem. There are birches, a river, "an old white horse," scrag and cliff below. Snow on the "morgue-dawn" is promised: a kind of death, presumably, but the world will be "myriad," which may mean multi-faceted, rich, and new as in Avison's sonnet "Snow." The vacationist asserts that she has not met anyone else in this new world but then speaks, paradoxically, of "their language." Whose language? The language of Rilke's angels? Of the visionary company of the past, those earlier mental travellers Herbert and

Blake and Hopkins and Emily Dickinson and Eliot? Of the new land, of the spirits of place, of northness? Whatever the case, it seems to be the speaker's task as visionary artist to learn this new language and to communicate it to those in more ordinary spaces.

"The Swimmer's Moment" also proposes some sort of surrender to a world beyond ordinary experience. Some invitation to enter that world comes to everyone, according to Avison, but many refuse it:

> By their refusal they are saved
> From the black pit, and also from contesting
> The deadly rapids, and emerging in
> The mysterious, and more ample, further waters.
> And so their bland-blank faces turn and turn
> Pale and forever on the rim of suction
> They will not recognize.

Those who do enter the whirlpool may achieve great inner riches even if they suffer outward defeat, but their achievement remains secret and dies with them. This is reminiscent of Klein's poet with his secret at the bottom of the sea or of novelist Morley Callaghan's "saints" with their dangerous inner compulsions. As in "The Valiant Vacationist," the problem of communicating such experience is stressed. Both poems remain vague about what precisely is happening (to the swimmer or climber) within the whirlpool or high up the stone steps: Eliot's whirlpool in *The Waste Land* and Yeats's winding stair or Eliot's staircase in "Ash Wednesday," for that matter, may have some part in this, though.

"Perspective" and "Snow" are more explicitly concerned with the subject of vision—both literal and spiritual vision. In "Perspective" the speaker begins by asking why it is that she sees, not as other people do, but as the Renaissance painter Mantegna did. Ordinary "seeing," she asserts boldly, is diseased; it cripples space. The perspective in which everything tapers to a point is an optical illusion: otherwise railway tracks, which look as if they are moving together, would meet. In the speaker's vision all objects, whether near or far, can be large and vivid, as they are in "primitive" art or a child's drawing in which things emotionally important are made larger:

> But ho you miss the impact of that fierce
> Raw boulder five miles off? You are not pierced
> By that great spear of grass on the horizon?
> You are not smitten with the shock
> Of that great thundering sky?

Here is a kind of zoom-lens effect in which a great spear of grass on the horizon can be seen. This is Paul Eluard's "other world" that is "in this one": the world that is literally marvellous if it is really looked at. The matter of scale is introduced as it was in the work of Birney, Klein and Layton. The tiny—the insects in Layton's poems, the insect in Avison's own "A Nameless One," or the living butterfly of her "Butterfly Bones" with his "world cut-diamond-eyed" and "fierce listening"—may be perceived as huge, as a universe in itself. This is an idea found in William Blake, of course, but in Avison and other Canadian poets it relates to the desire to expand the consciousness, the dwarfed self, to fill the vast spaces to be dwarf and giant both:

> when we clanged
> Into the vasty station we were indeed
> Brave companmy for giants.

But safety and sanity demand restrictions, limits, order. Men cannot live exclusively in a visionary world. Avison admits sadly that fear of the world makes man inclined to "press out dwindling vistas" from the massive flux Mantegna knew. This is something like the receding perspective of Philip Bentley's drawings in Sinclair Ross's classic novel *As for Me and My House* and his later tentative escape into larger spaces and rhythms. It is a Canadian problem, sometimes expressed in terms of the garrison and the open space, and the solution would seem to be some version of Avison's (or Layton's or Purdy's) shifting perspective; that is, Canadians must live in those physical and mental enclosures and sets that are necessary for survival and at the same time venture forth imaginatively into the open. It is obvious now that Canadians have been too timid and too self-enclosed in the past and that they must live in the larger world that is their fate, but at the same time they must protect and preserve themselves. It is the balance that matters. It is not the garrison *against* the wilderness so much as the garrison *and* the wilderness, the two balanced both literally and imaginatively. It is possible to live in several worlds at once or to be two (or more) men at once, as Al Purdy put it. After all, Margaret Avison seems to suggest, the development of rules of perspective was just as wonderful an adventure for Mantegna and his successors as the liberation from them can be for us. Salvation would seem to lie in rapid movement, for Avison—another follower of Heraclitus—as for Layton and Purdy.
    Linear order can imprison us:

> Strait thinking set us down in rows
> and rigged the till.

If, with dainty stepping, we unbox ourselves
while still Explosion slumbers,
putting aside mudcakes,
the buying, selling, trucking, packaging
of mudcakes,
sun-stormed, daring to gambol,
might there not be an immense answering
of human skies?
a new expectant largeness?
Form has its flow,
a Heraclitus-river with no riverbank
we can play poise on now.

"Intra-Political"

This call to imaginative freedom from the limitations of the childish commercial mentality and from the obsession to order everything in masculine linear fashion is radical in the truest sense. There is an immense curving world out there that is normally never seen.

The sonnet "Snow" begins with the now-famous lines:

Nobody stuffs the world in at your eyes.
The optic heart must venture: a jail-break
And re-creation.

The speaker then proceeds to give herself over to what seems to be deliberate hallucination, shaping the process and experience of sight quite consciously. Inner and outer worlds are joined as the snow becomes sedges, wild rice, rivery pewter, cinders, rhizomes, candy-bright disks, asters: it is verbal cinema again, as in Klein and Purdy. Images of the organic break through the sterility of white snow, suggesting perhaps that all things constitute one organism. This is metamorphosis, as in Klein's poem "Lone Bather"; it is the kind of vision or "see-ing" that Lampman, an earlier sonneteer, could not quite articulate. The world, says the poet, is "desolate," deathly, uncreative, if the soul cannot perceive in this larger way. Yet death remains real in any case, and it is part of the message of the visionary world, a necessary part of the process, of "creation's unseen freight." There is pain, too, in the pleasure of imagination and the re-creation of the world. The "listener" may be changed, may receive a return (his "change") from the expenditure of the imagination in the world (a commerce very different from the packaging and buying of "mudcakes"), but he will also be "sad." The poet, Klein's nth Adam who collaborates in

God's continuous creation of the world, brings pain as well as pleasure and the liberation or "jail-break" from old mental and perceptual habits.

"New Year's Poem" articulates a point of rest or balance, an interface between interior and open space, human and outer worlds:

>   the long loop of winter wind
> Smoothing its arc from dark Arcturus down
> To the bricked corner of the drifted courtyard,
> And the still windowledge.
>   Gentle and just pleasure
> It is, being human, to have won from space
> This unchill, habitable interior.

The "still windowledge" is the centre of the poet's meditation. Inside is space organized for human purposes, human safety; outside a vast, seemingly limitless universe. It is the Canadian situation in a nutshell.

Man's desire for freedom and his need to order co-exist eternally. In "The Iconoclasts," Avison suggests that new order, particularly the new order of new art, is born from ferocity, from a wildness within that corresponds to the wilderness without. The impossible problem continues forever, however, as old adventures solidify into old order, and new beginnings are endlessly made. This means, among other things, that man's identity is ever flexible and fluid, something Purdy seems also to know very well.

The solution to the eternal problem is, for Avison as for Klein, the religious one in which all things become possible:

> In the mathematics of God
> there are percentages beyond one hundred.
>
> His new creation is
> One, whole, and a
> beginning.

"First"

Creation is whole and yet is always beginning, always new, as it is perceived: only the language of paradox can render this truth.

Margaret Avison's later poetry, which is collected in *The Dumbfounding*, the book that follows her conversion to Christianity, is even more extraordinary than her earlier intricate experimentation with traditional form and rhetoric. Her sense of the artist's "religious" function is much deeper and more humble. Poems like "Black-White under Green,""The Absorbed," and "Searching and Sounding" have a freedom and flow and a driving energy that are comparable to Purdy's, though completely different in tone. They are also more sensuous and concrete than some of her earlier poems:

> The inside breathing here
> closes down all the window but a visor-slit
> on the night glare.
>   New cold is
> in dry-thorn nostrils.
>
> Alone, he plays, still there. We
> struggle, our animal fires
> pitted against those
> several grape-white stars,
> their silence.
>
>   "The Absorbed"

Here the Canadian situation of struggle is felt as intensely as in Pratt, whose energy Avison would seem to have inherited; the surprising but appropriate "grape-white stars" is an effect very much her own. And in "Searching and Sounding," in which the speaker is pursued by her version of the Hound of Heaven, there is an emotional power and an immediacy one did not find in the early poems.

The Canadian fascination with space-time may lead to a fascination with light:

> In July this early sky is
> a slope-field, a tangled
> shining—blue-green, moist, in
> heaped up pea-vines, in milk-hidden
> tendrils, in light so strong
> it seems a shadow of
> further light, were the heart
> large enough to find its succulence
> and feed and not be glutted there.
>
>   "Searching and Sounding"

In this poem Avison finds Jesus not alone in the vision of light, as she had expected, but

> in the sour air
> of a morning-after rooming-house hall-bedroom;

not in Gethsemane's grass, perfumed with prayer,
but here,
seeking to cool the gray-stubbled cheek
    and the filth-choked throat
    and the scalding self-loathing heart, and
failing, for he is
sick,
for I. . . .

It is in identification with the world's outcasts that one finds Christ:

I am he
    or I am
a babbling boy
aged twenty, mentally distracted, blunted
by sedatives and too-long innocence
without your hand, teaching his the ax-heft or
    throttle-bar or
    grease-monkey's gun or
        any craft or art.

The way to fuller vision and harmony involves, for Avison, a descent to "The place/of jackals. . .howling among the tombs." But Christ's descent redeems evolution (as it does for Pratt):

that the remotest fishrib,
the hairiest pink-thing there
might as one fragment
make towards the fullness you
put off, there, on the
ravening shore I view, from
my gull-blanched cliffs,
and shiver.
GATHER my fragments towards
the radium, the
all-swallowing moment
once more.

"Dwarf" that she is, the poet clings to the little light she can bear, and asks for the ultimate union with the whole.
    An extraordinary poet from the beginning—"Perspective" was written in

1940—she has become ever more extraordinary and significant over the years. With Purdy, she is probably the most important English-Canadian poet.

In fact, these two poets have, in their separate ways, developed a genuinely Canadian idiom. It is one appropriate to a country of stretching space and shifting perspective, an organic and flexible form, an idiom never too strict or free to accommodate the poet's individual growth and movement. R.G. Everson, Souster, and Dudek certainly have contributed to this development, but Purdy and Avison have, in their best work, perfected it. Many of our poets have been specialists or else are eclectic and versatile to a degree that inhibits the discovery of a deeper voice or voices. Purdy and Avison have gone beyond eclecticism to create this voice.

Facts and Dreams Again

Two other poets who have over the years developed an impressive individuality provide an interesting contrast: Milton Acorn, Al Purdy's friend and the most radical socialist and nationalist poet in Canada, as well as the poetic historian and interpreter of Prince Edward Island, as Purdy has been of Ontario and beyond, and P.K. Page, who turned from a species of Marxism to a religious exploration and an extraordinary stress on "vision" that links her to Klein and Avison. By and large, Acorn is a poet of fact, like Purdy, and Page a poet of dream, like Avison; however, all the best poets tend, at their best, to transcend these boundaries, and Avison and Purdy in particular seem able to move between the two worlds with grace and ease.

One of the most impressive of Acorn's many poetic virtues is directness:

> If this brain's over-tempered
> consider that the fire was want
> and the hammers were fists.
> I've tasted my blood too much
> to love what I was born to.
>
> But my mother's look
> was a field of brown oats, soft-bearded;
> her voice rain and air rich with lilacs:
> and I loved her too much to like
> how she dragged her days like a sled over gravel.
>
> "I've tasted my blood"

There is no inhibition or embarrassment here in the direct expression of anger and love. Acorn can put lyricism to the service of social comment. Great tenderness and great indignation co-exist in his work, making it evident that it is indeed written out of love, not simply out of paranoia. Acorn sings of working men and women and their lives, and in his love poems celebrates the autonomy and independence of the beloved. There is in his language a certain resemblance to Purdy's utterance, on the one hand, and to Layton's, on the other, born, probably, of their association in Montreal, but the early Acorn's language is usually rockier, his expression more terse. Still, the later poems in *More Poems for People* are looser in structure as well as more openly militant in their socialism and nationalism; they ramble on discursively, preaching Canadian liberation from capitalism and from the United States. Robin Mathews is the only other Canadian poet who pursues this mission equally stridently, and he lacks Acorn's technical skills. So, in a sense, Acorn stands alone, and is apparently pleased to do so.

His individuality is paradoxically and sometimes rather curiously in evidence in his 1977 collection *Jackpine Sonnets,* which is something of a new departure in that it attempts to revitalize the sonnet form, as Robert Lowell did elsewhere, without the hindrance of conventional strictures of rhyme, metre, and length. Lampman, Klein, Kenneth Leslie, and others are invoked as Canadian sonneteers of public utterance. Acorn himself seems gradually to have moved away from an earlier concreteness of statement and image, partly out of a desire to make larger and more general political and social statements and partly because of the fascination with technique that is apparent in all his work. He is concerned with the creative fiddling with "rhymes, internal, external, assonances, vowel rhymes, consonant rhymes, and something I call a thought-rhyme. . .plus rhythm-rhymes" and "the alexandrine twelve-syllable line. . .eight-syllable, seven-syllable, even five-syllable lines."[1] He has become more formal and less an imagist. I find the best of his sonnets impressive, even if they are (like Lowell's) a little stupefying in the mass. They do not, of course, aspire to that flexible organic flow achieved in the best of Avison and Purdy; instead they have a deliberated, formal air (a little reminiscent of the flavour of A.J.M. Smith's rather more orthodox sonnets) that offers a different kind of pleasure to the reader sensitive to this kind of craftsmanship.

Acorn's approach to life and art is complemented by the inner exploration of a P.K. Page. Though very individual, she is yet another of those Canadian poets who move into interior landscapes:

> In a pit
> figures the size of pins are strangely lit
> and might be dancing but you know they're not.
> Like Dante's vision of the nether hell

men struggle with the bright cold fires of salt,
locked in the black inferno of the rock:
the filter here, not innocence but guilt.

                    "Photos of a Salt Mine"

These people in a circle on the sand
are dark against its gold
turn like a wheel
revolving in a horizontal plane

.   .   .   .

I see them there in three dimensions yet
their height implies another space

.   .   .   .

all their movements make a compass rose
surging and altering.

                    "Another Space"

Inferno and paradise: these quotations reveal the dimensions of P.K. Page's imaginative universe. At one pole a vision of hell shading into social concern; at the other a mandala expressing harmony and wholeness, like Dante's multifoliate rose. In "Photos of a Salt Mine" a picture of innocence and beauty gives way to a vision of evil. In "Another Space" what appears to be a "primitive" ritual dance expresses the ultimate wholeness and harmony of a universe that is forever "surging and altering" and yet forever one. A reference to Chagall suggests a Chassidic dance.

"Most of my poems," P.K. Page has written, "have been doors closing. A few were doors opening."[2] In this smaller group she includes "Another Space" along with "Arras" and "Stories of Snow." All of these particular poems involve journeys into inner space—through and behind the eye. Like Avison, Page is an explorer.

Her earliest poems are poems of social observation, but very different from Acorn's. They are poems which yoke together an obviously genuine compassion, especially for girls and women, but also, in one instance, for homosexuals, and more generally for all those who suffer alienation in contemporary society, with a somewhat too decorative metaphoric busyness and much alliteration. It is to a large extent the period style of the 1940's, the kind of neo-Freudian-neo-Marxist-Auden-Thomas rococo that leads to this kind of facile label. This does not, of course, do any justice to the best of the poems—to the remarkable "The Stenographers," for instance. And her style becomes sharper, cleaner, more refined and more definitively her own as time goes on.

Page once specialized in poems about the loss of childhood innocence and security (for example, "The Bands and the Beautiful Children"), case-histories of neurotic childhoods, and in some cases, neurotic lives, and more positive suggestions of the theme of illness turned to beauty. In "Images of Angels," a witty poem about the loss of visionary faculty in the modern world, she seems to reach beyond the depiction of social flaws and psychological problems to an examination of the deeper roots of these in the atrophied human imagination. In so doing she enters her "other space," a larger dimension of perception and being. This is a natural tendency of twentieth-century thought and art. Behind and beyond the highly useful analyses of Marx and Freud is a larger realm of understanding whose nature was perhaps best articulated by Carl Jung. Now that psychology and physiology, art, meditation, and a number of other disciplines are beginning to be combined once again as parts of one science, the much longed for re-discovery of the psyche, that is, of the whole body-mind in its whole relationship to the universe, may well be at hand. Page's rather pathetic angels would then become like Rilke's angels, at home in all worlds.

Interior worlds make themselves ever more strongly felt in Page's later poems. Metaphors are now more consistently and simply symbolic rather than gaudy and self-serving. She presents personal landscapes and landscapes of love lost or very difficult, a white "landscape without love," contrasted white and green, male and female landscapes. Lovers turn one another to water, to stone or mineral. In the difficult "Arras" the speaker apparently feels the stillness of death in the cold perfection of art and seeks to alter it with vivid life. A peacock insinuates itself into the scene through the poet's eye.

There are a number of poems enlarging upon the themes of the power of metaphor to transform reality and the power of the human imagination to extend itself into the cosmos in a new direction, another space, in spite of physical decline and death. There is considerable emphasis on "see-ing." The poet is seer. Page has written of A.M. Klein, whom she knew in Montreal in 1944, that she was struck that "for all his acceptance of ideological and psychological theory, he seemed to reach beyond both to a larger reality. And this, though I comprehended it only vaguely, I recognized as real."[3] She too became a religious poet. Her "see-ing" can be compared to that of Margaret Avison or to that of Margaret Atwood or Gwendolyn MacEwen in the next generation. Atwood in particular seems to have picked up a great deal both from Avison and Page as well as from Jay Macpherson, whose visionary world seems, however, much more self-enclosed and literary.

Page's style has been refined and perfected as her insight into the nature of her experience has clarified. She has learned to deploy rhyme, image and sound-effect and to move lightly in and out of a basic iambic pentameter line with unobtrusive skill. As poet and calligrapher she delights in exotic details and images, but she has learned as Klein did to subordinate whimsy to the microcosmic design or large metaphor that captures a sense of the macrocosm. This makes it necessary to go beyond normal seeing:

> And choir me too to keep my heart a size
> larger than seeing, unseduced by each
> bright glimpse of beauty striking like a bell,
> so that the whole may toll,
> its meaning shine
> clear of the myriad images that still—
> do what I will—encumber its pure line.

"After Rain"

P.K. Page is cool and contemplative; sometimes her sense of cosmic harmony, enhanced by the study of Sufism, may dispose rather too easily of the gritty social problems addressed more directly by Acorn and Purdy and even at times by Avison the social worker, as well as of the general problem of evil. Similarly, in her work there is a whole universe but not necessarily one that is always beginning; her forms are never so open as those of Avison and Purdy. But her work provides access to a rich world of the imagination. She is one of the most notable visionaries in Canadian poetry.

Notes

1. Letters in the author's possession.
2. John Robert Colombo, ed., *How Do I Love Thee?* (Edmonton: Hurtig, 1970), p. 27.
3. P.K. Page, "The Sense of Angels," *Jewish Dialog,* Passover 1973.

Poets of a Certain Age

If Avison and Purdy and Acorn and Page are major inheritors and developers of a Canadian tradition and also the likeliest progenitors of new developments of interest, there are other fine and important voices of the 1950's and since who cannot be ignored. They are a varied lot but may be described as poets of a certain age—not yet venerable—who are also inheritors of the Canadian experience and the various approaches past poets have taken to it, and whose work, which is for the most part quieter and less urgent than that either of their immediate elders or of the young poets and poet-novelists who achieved such swift acclaim and attention in the exhilarating 1960's, is still quietly in process.

A good deal has been said of mountaineers or poets of fact (Roberts, Lampman, Pratt, F.R. Scott, Birney, Purdy, Souster, Acorn, Nowlan, Newlove); of swimmers or poets of dream (Carman, Smith, Klein, Page, Layton, Reaney, Macpherson, Mandel, Cohen, Ondaatje, MacEwen, Atwood); and of those who often combine the two (D.C. Scott, Purdy, Avison, Atwood). Presumably, all poets aspire to the last condition, and probably all achieve it in their best poems, but most tend to lean more or less consistently in one direction or the other. Sometimes there are pairs of poets that complement one another in this way: Roberts and Carman, Scott and Smith, Souster and Layton.

In Smith, as sometimes in Carman, the poetry of dream is structured by classical myth. More recently, a loose group of poets—principally James Reaney, Jay Macpherson, and the earlier Eli Mandel—have found the critical theories of Northrop Frye, with their emphasis on archetypes and structural patterns in literature, to be a convenient and congenial conceptual framework for the expression of their highly individual sensibilities.

Reaney, who has written plays as well as poems, is the most prolific and highly acclaimed of these "mythopoeic" poets.

Reaney's work, however, is quite uneven. His is an exceedingly willful and eccentric talent—so much so that the theories of Frye, or some other theories, or else the discipline of working with actors and the inevitable constrictions of the stage are essential to him if he is to direct his remarkable and energetic gifts. Nevertheless, he has grown as an artist; it looks now as if he is becoming the first really original and successful playwright writing in English in Canada.

Reaney, like Smith, has written a number of very good poems. The early poems of *The Red Heart* and before have a wicked, whimsical flavour that is uniquely their own. When they work, as most do, they are marvellous; when they do not, they are merely coy. The loss of childhood innocence in western Ontario is a recurrent theme, and the child's-eye view is vividly rendered. Like Smith, Reaney was, it seems, influenced by Edith Sitwell, but in this latter case the Sitwellian whimsy does not interfere with a sense of Canada. The farmboy gets lost in the paper world of the Katzenjammer Kids and the childhood world of the school globe, which gives way, however, to another world of adult horrors, violence, and sex, which is seen here as something nasty and degrading. Reaney has something in common with Leonard Cohen (in his Peter Pan mood) here. These poems might also be read alongside George Elliott's stories in *The Kissing Man*, where those trapped in a dull, philistine place seek for some hidden magic. Time haunts the protagonist of these poems; in the very striking "Dark Lagoon" the tick-tock of the mother's heart is already prophesying the ultimate death of the child who is still in the womb. Other poems (for example, "The Great Lakes Suite," "Rewards for Ambitious Trees") have a pleasant craziness and a charming insignificance that is hard to resist.

This zaniness becomes visionary in Reaney's next phase, however, producing not only striking passages but also much willful obscurity and sub-Blakean doggerel. Reaney had not found a way fully to communicate the religious vision that now overwhelmed him. There is in all this, though, a recognizable suggestion of both personal and general apocalypse. What follows, Reaney's most ambitious attempt to communicate this vision, is a western Ontario version of Spenser's *Shepherd's Calendar* with a cast of farm geese.

A Suit of Nettles will never be to most readers' taste in spite of Northrop Frye's praise. There is self-conscious and rather wearying technical virtuosity; there is a very amusing attack on the puritan severities of F.R. Leavis; and there is a moving conclusion in which another dimension of existence ("another space"), one that transcends the ring or "round" of personal and general history, is suggested. But too much of the poem is precious word play.

Twelve Letters to a Small Town restores the more mundane, ironic, and charming perspective of Reaney's earliest poems. "To the Avon River" is one of his finest and most successful pieces. One of its implications is that Reaney has come to perceive the need for a Canadian language and movement in poetry. He says to the river, which is very different from Shakespeare's Avon, that he would like to flow "like you." Such an ambition is rarely achieved in his own work, since he seems to be addicted to traditional nursery rhyme and to chant, but in this particular poem there is a beautiful, smooth flow.

Reaney's real technical development, however, has come through his work in the theatre. As Leonard Cohen became a novelist, Reaney became a playwright—surely a courageous enterprise in a country that then had virtually no life of the theatre of its own. Over the years he has grown enormously as a dramatist, partly because he has been able to write parts with particular actors in mind. While most of Reaney's early verse-plays will probably prove to be no more genuinely theatrical than those of Eliot or Auden, his recent trilogy "The Donnellys" is a magnificent achievement. Reaney's love of chant and ritual has been combined with a feel for imaginative stage-business and an effective manipulation of several planes of time in his dramatic narrative, so that past and present are juxtaposed in a kind of eternal present. The trilogy brings nineteenth-century Ontario vividly to life, creating a myth of our violent forefathers that may be set beside Al Purdy's or Margaret Laurence's re-visioning of the past.

Reaney's work, various, ambitious, rich, and uneven as it has been, invites comparison with that of a number of other important Canadian writers working in rather disparate areas of the Canadian and the human reality. Jay Macpherson's is a much more contained, limited, and controlled talent, and for that reason her intricate and beautiful lyrics defy any obvious technical criticism. The microcosmic universe of *The Boatman* is a world of traditional myths and tales, itself a kind of grammar of myth inspired by Northrop Frye, to whom the book is dedicated. (Reaney's poems too may be seen as models of the universe, as designed by Frye: the critical theorist as God.) Macpherson's angle of vision, which encompasses "these poor children/Ruined from the womb" ("Poor Child"), is not unlike Reaney's. Her world too is a fallen one of separated sexes and a remembered, possibly pre-natal Eden or lost heroic age. But Eden lives on in the mind of the sleeper, or poet, in all of us, the sleeping giant who is, presumably, the collective consciousness of mankind at large. Consciousness itself is an ark that carries all creation inside it. Macpherson's fisherman—another version of the poet, this time as active or redeeming consciousness—angles in the lake of his own and the world's darkness until he is eventually "hoicked" in himself by God. It is a book (or boat) full of rich and suggestive images and beasts (like Klein's beasts or Yeats's circus animals, only more tightly organized and domesticated), from which younger poets, particularly MacEwen and Atwood, have obviously benefited.

The most notable thing about the early poems of Eli Mandel is that while he also employs classical and Old Testament myth to depict a horrific, fallen world, he appears to reject as unreal the transcendent vision of Reaney and Macpherson. There seems to be a note of scepticism in the interrogative conclusion of his tribute to the model-building of these two poets:

> What boxed bird so great
> it can eat
> stone, man, star and seed?

> "A Cage of Oats"

Again, Mandel's "mythopoeic" poems are more obviously grounded in immediate and autobiographical experience—his labyrinth a university building, his Daedalus a man tinkering with a car in the garage, his David a boy (with poems aching in his head) out after gophers with a slingshot. The general atmosphere of horror presumably has much of its origin in the experience of war. And it seems quite inevitable that Mandel should increasingly direct his gift for unusual images and observations to social comment—references to Vietnam and to figures of pop myth are more frequent in the later work, as they are in Leonard Cohen's poems. What is consistent from first to last is the sense of the world's horror and the "madness" that can resist it; it is a forceful and disturbing vision despite, perhaps because of, the elegance of the writing. Having, it seems, resisted Frye's system, Mandel presents a world that is open—as Cohen's is, as Avison's or Purdy's is, though Mandel seems to lack their religious sense—not one ordered in such a way that all is settled, if only in the head. Even the imagination is in constant flux here. Consequently, while Jay Macpherson's world is perfectly self-enclosed, a marvellous jewel-box or small perfection and Reaney has been able to liberate himself from a self-enclosed and frequently obscure poetry only by turning to drama, Mandel seems to have the potential to develop further as a poet.

Phyllis Gotlieb is another poet interested in myth and pop myth, but not one to be overwhelmed by anyone's theories about it. The world of her poems is one of whimsical play and driving nervous energy. The poet revels in both the ordinary and the mythic, which she tends to reduce to the ordinary, often very humorously. Everything becomes play; in good Jewish fashion, Gotlieb questions God, Death, and the other large and frightening realities about their competence, morals, and intentions. A kind of verbal slapstick is often her strategy for dealing with the terrible. It would seem that she sees life as a show, a more or less absurd circus or carnival, the ultimate meaning of which is impossible to fathom.

D.G. Jones's concerns are more metaphysical than mythical; he is possessed by the Canadian interest in space as well as by the problem of man's relationship to the non-human that surrounds his clumsy and sometimes suicidal attempts at civilization. He writes extremely well of birds and animals in the busy outdoors, capturing that sense of mystery in the non-human that any attentive watcher feels. Indeed, his descriptive poetry of the outdoors may well be the most objective (that is, participatory) of all the poets. Man's loneliness as a "language" animal aware of his own mortality, of the transience of all things, is stressed, most beautifully in the long poem "Soliloquy to Absent Friends." There is a sense of disorientation in a drifting, dissolving world, which deepens in Jones's later poems as it is blended with a sly survival humour. The poet appears as a rueful survivor, aware and ironic, able to continue in his love for a unobliging and shifty world, surrendering to process, like Purdy. Technically, Jones's poems are notable for exactitude, for a precise and elegant diction and lining that has probably influenced the even more laconic style of Margaret Atwood. Such earlier "metaphysicals" as Smith and Glassco have obviously influenced Jones.

Fred Cogswell, like his fellow Maritime realists (or poets of fact) Alden Nowlan and Elizabeth Brewster, writes well about people and about love. Indeed, he creates a whole world of New Brunswick and its people, an orderly world of the stunted strong, of puritan and sensualist in conflict, in orderly, traditional forms. His Maritimes recall Edward Arlington Robinson's New England. As it happens, Nowlan and Brewster have attracted more attention than Cogswell, perhaps because they work, for the most part, with freer forms. Nowlan's poems are also notably darker and more fearful than Cogswell's; this may strike a deeper chord in the souls of those who endure and enjoy a harsh and lovely land. If Cogswell is a Robinson for New Brunswick, one with considerable insight into the nature of erotic experience, Nowlan is closer to Robert Frost, even if less cagey and ironic than that most "Canadian" of Americans. His is a magic realism in which the depths of consciousness can be seen at work. He is aware of the terror at the heart of the world as well as highly appreciative of sensual joy, a balance found in more recent poets like David Helwig and John Newlove as well. Neither Cogswell nor Nowlan is concerned with myth as poetic structure to the degree than Reaney and Macpherson have been. Indeed,

Nowlan's poems derive their movement from an emotional power greater than that of most Canadian poets.

Elizabeth Brewster, the third member of this realistic Maritime school, is also the quietest, but her apparent straightforwardness is deceptive. Such a steady gaze and competence as hers makes it possible to deal with a wide range of subjects, characters, and realities. Her world—like Cogswell's and Nowlan's—may seem restricted in one way, but the range of her attention is immense; it takes in a good deal of past and contemporary human experience. Brewster is usually objective, contemplative, wise. At times, particularly in rhyming love poems, she seems somewhat like Jay Macpherson, but her most characteristic work is unrhymed and unmetrical. She is, like her colleagues, very good at writing about people, both ordinary people and extraordinary ones like D.H. Lawrence and Dag Hammerskjold.

Most of the poets discussed so far in this arbitrary grouping, with the exceptions of Nowlan and perhaps Cogswell, have been more reflective or intellectual than really passionate in their singing. There are other accomplished poets—including Ronald Bates, Douglas Lochhead, Robert Gibbs, and Marya Fiamengo, and such gifted settlers as Walter Bauer, Kenneth McRobbie, Peter Miller, David Knight, Christopher Levenson, Henry Beissel, Stanley Cooperman, Francis Sparshott, Mike Doyle, and Robin Skelton—who seem excessively civilized, though the late Cooperman, who was beginning to move in new directions, did let out the odd barbaric yawp. Perhaps the epitome of the cool and rational Canadian poet, though, is Daryl Hine, Leonard Cohen's contemporary at McGill, who has also made himself a name in the United States and has been editor of *Poetry*. His first book was dedicated to Jay Macpherson and praised by Northrop Frye. And, indeed, Hine is, in his own way, an excellent poet—quite classical and austere enough to gladden the heads of A.J.M. Smith and others in the Apollonian wing of Canadian poetry. He has wit, an Audenesque facility and grace with traditional forms and even, sometimes, a power that creates a degree of emotional empathy.

Still, it is curious that these poets are so cool—especially after Layton and the others of his generation. Are there not any poets a little older than Leonard Cohen who are bizarre and passionate instead of just mildly crazy? The two poets who complete the group of poets of a certain age may just fit the bill. They are Joan Finnigan and Phyllis Webb.

Joan Finnigan is as close to being a wholly "natural" writer as any poet Canada has. Possessed of a vigorous, robust, expansive, and passionate (though not bizarre) disposition, she paints with broad and sometimes sloppy brushstrokes. Her free-verse style recalls Purdy's, though she is not usually so much in control either of her style or of her sentimentality. But the bonus—when the poems do work, and often even in poems that are flawed—is an emotional power not found in the cooler and quieter, more intellectual poets. Finnigan is a shrewd observer of people; she writes of emotional hunger in a world of insufficient love.

Phyllis Webb is much more the craftswoman, and what she articulates so precisely is a very bleak view of the world. Her "poet in his tree of hell" can "see life steadily and see it well" ("In Situ"). She perceives a world in which people are made beautiful only to be broken, a world whose logic is that of a madhouse designed for the insane human race. Here, her vision might be compared to Mandel's or Cohen's; they also see the world as a mad labyrinth. Everything vanishes in time and in the evolutionary process, and Webb laments the passing of things in poems which are both witty and passionate. A fine formal control is maintained even in poems that articulate states near the edge of insanity, and this gives some of the poems remarkable tension. For sanity, for stability, the poet turns to "making" that is, craft, to the precise observation of small events and moments. In her "Naked Poems," perhaps the most beautiful love poems to have been written in Canada (quite aside from the interesting fact that the lovers are both women) and certainly the most successful "minimal" poems that have been produced, she celebrates love, even if it be transient. The room, the moment of beauty in isolation from the world, is captured in brief, precise lines of immaculate clarity.

Sophisticated craft—this is certainly to be found in the best work of these poets. Perhaps most of them, like the poets of the 1920's, err on the side of caution. And then again, perhaps this is not error, given the explosion of poetic experiment and general thrashing about that occurs in the next generation. The poets of a certain age continue to set a good example, to provide formal models for the turbulent, questing young.

It is good that they are there; when they themselves began, there were only a few good poets in the country, but now there are hundreds of potentially fine poets who can do with some instruction from their most accomplished elders. The achievement of the older poets is as considerable as that of any in the contemporary English-speaking world (even if it is little known outside our borders, in the old and new imperial centres where publicity dwells). There is much energy, variety, life, and originality in their work, and in some of it perhaps an implicit realization as well of the deluge that was to follow. A new vision or Beast can be seen lurking somewhere behind and within the structural framework adopted by those poets influenced by Frye's theories, behind and within the freelance myth-making of other poets, in the darkness at the heart of the realistic world of the Maritime poets, in the articulate despair and celebration of Nowlan and Jones and Webb. Their work also reflects some of the new directions, the new multiplicity of vision emerging in the ongoing explorations of Purdy, Avison and Page. Indeed, all Canadian poets of whatever age who are still writing are now part of the deluge.

This explosion or deluge or confusion of tongues—in both prose and poetry—is itself, whatever the problems it poses for critics and readers, an evidence of growth in the collective consciousness. It indicates that many have gone down into the dark and returned, that much that was dark in Canada is now coming into the light.

PART FOUR

Quest into Darkness: The Poet-Novelists

The Lake of Darkness

Douglas LePan's Roving Picket

The modern Canadian poet-novelist is largely a phenomenon of the 1960's and 1970's. This would seem to reflect the opening-up of possibilities for Canadian writers and the growth in national consciousness that one associates with this time. The advent of an unprecedented number of accomplished new novelists who are not poets is a related development. It seems significant that a number of poets of this generation have not been content to be poets only, and that others, who have written little or no fiction, have attempted ambitious long poems, many of them concerned with Canadian history, as if they were attempting to re-do Pratt's work in terms more meaningful to later sensibilities and attitudes. Canadian poets have once again been attempting larger structures, a fuller exploration of inner and outer worlds.

The extension into fiction is of special interest. To be sure, Crawford, Campbell, Roberts, D.C. Scott, and others wrote fiction. Some of it, like Roberts's animal stories, is rather interesting; most of it, thoroughly forgettable. And many of our poets of the twentieth century have written fiction, sometimes of a non-realistic or striking and original kind. Some examples are A.M. Klein's novella *The Second Scroll*, P.K. Page's romantic tales, John Glassco's erotica, Phyllis Gotlieb's science fiction, and George Bowering's more spaced-out stories à la Kerouac. A few poets, among them Birney, Souster, Brewster, Nowlan, and Bowering, have written whole novels of a more conventional kind. Sometimes, as with Birney's *Turvey*, the novel provides a further and larger development of an aspect of the poet's sensibility. But few of these practitioners, however skilful, can be regarded as having extended the thematic, formal, and expressive possibilities of fiction in Canada in the way that such poets of the sixties as Leonard Cohen, Margaret Atwood, and Michael Ondaatje have done, though Bowering might yet prove to be another such. And Robert Kroetsch might be cited as a rather special case, a novelist-poet whose novels have become more bizarre as he has taken to writing documentary poems.

There is no doubt that simply by doing it the older poet-novelists have provided example and inspiration to the younger ones. And one of them, a possible exception to the remarks above about the extension of fictional possibilities, may have been especially influential. For surely Leonard Cohen, inspiration of many young poets and novelists alike, took note of the way his poetic ancestor A.M. Klein had adapted the method of James Joyce to his own use. Indeed, Klein's Zionist quest-romance *The Second Scroll* (1951) is a special case of the poet's novel in Canada. It combines prose and poetry in a way that is exciting if not wholly successful, since some passages, such as "Gloss Gimel," a magnificent prose-poem and meditation on the paintings of the Sistine Chapel, are so much more striking and powerful than others that the whole is somewhat unbalanced. But the novel builds nevertheless an imposing symbolic and allegorical structure around its brilliant moments. No doubt Cohen looked beyond Klein to the general development of the symbolic novel in the twentieth century, but in *Beautiful Losers* there are aims, methods, virtues, and faults akin to those of *The Second Scroll*. Each provides a symbolic portrait of a people anguished and fragmented but dreaming of unity. Each is itself a poet's novel of brilliant fragments, whose whole effect is greater than the sum of its uneven parts, as if to prove that poets rarely have the patience required for the careful and detailed development of realistic or documentary action with well-realized social context and fully rounded characters, but that a symbolic structure and a compressed expression come naturally to them.

The young Michael Ondaatje's admiration for *Beautiful Losers* is recorded in his book on Leonard Cohen, in which he calls the novel "gorgeous and brave." Obviously, *Beautiful Losers* offers one precedent for the violence, exotica, and fragmented narrative of his own *Collected Works of Billy the Kid*. Another of Ondaatje's enthusiasms, however, leads us back to an almost equally bizarre and poetic novel by a writer not usually regarded as a poet: Sheila Watson's *The Double Hook* (1959). Like *The Second Scroll*, it is a special case, much admired by Margaret Atwood as well as by Michael Ondaatje, and thus another notable forerunner of the poet's novel of the 1960's and 1970's.

Indeed, in a sense *The Double Hook* is itself a prose-poem, so vivid, sensuous, and metaphorical is its language. The utterances of Coyote, moreover, are even arranged in short, free-verse lines. Thus, Sheila Watson may be seen as another kind of poet-novelist;[1] which serves as a reminder that some of the most influential giants of modern fiction in English—particularly Joyce, Lawrence, Faulkner, and Virginia Woolf, who pioneered the fiction of inner being—were in the same sense poets in the novel, though only one of them, Lawrence, was also a great poet. Certainly these writers helped to blur the boundaries and to make possible the highly symbolic or visionary fiction of such as Laurence Durrell, Malcolm Lowry, Jack Kerouac, Patrick White, or Ernest Buckler, thereby providing an international context in which a poet might aspire to the larger expression of his vision in fictional form. But this happens in a notable way in Canadian literature, (excluding the non-Canadian Lowry, as I think we must) only with such sports as *The Second Scroll* and *The Double Hook* and then with the advent of poet-novelists Cohen, Ondaatje, MacEwen, Atwood, and others of the nationalistic 1960's and 1970's, when the old task of articulating Canadians' psychic experience of the new world assumed a new urgency.

The Double Hook is set in the Cariboo country, a world in which the beauty and the terror of elemental forces are held in balance. The ghost of old Mrs. Potter, whose murder generates the action, is seen fishing, but not for fish. She also holds up her lamp in broad daylight. She is questioning the land even after her death, as Atwood's Susanna Moodie will do, but it yields up no answers, only an equal amount of beauty and terror. There is an extraordinary stress on vision in the novel as there is in the poems of Page, MacEwen, and Atwood, but the vision reflects the Canadian ambivalence. Both the glory and the darkness (or D.C. Scott's "beauty of peace" and "beauty of terror") must be accepted as given, since Leviathan cannot be captured with a bent pin. He who fishes for glory hooks the darkness too: it is a lesson of much Canadian literature, including Birney's "David," to take an obvious example. The inscrutable Coyote, symbolic embodiment of the power and the unpredictable trickiness of the elements, presides over death and birth here. An Indian demi-god is the appropriate expression of the spirit of place for the white man too. Sharing the experience of place instead of hiding behind barriers, garrisons of fear, is seen here too as a way to true community. Eventually, in death or in the minds of the surviving and reviving community, the old woman gives up her attempt to force vision and becomes one with the place, sinking true roots:

> I saw James Potter's old mother standing by my brown pool, he said. I was thinking of catching some fish for the lot of us. But she wasn't fishing, he said. Just standing like a tree, with its roots reaching out to water (NCL, pp. 117-18).

The mystery—the beauty and the terror, the glory and the darkness—must be accepted if man is to live and be at home here. Later Margaret Atwood echoes Watson when she writes of Indian gods and parental ghosts in *Surfacing*, of the pioneer fishing for a great vision in "Progressive

Insanities of a Pioneer,'' and of the old woman who is resurrected as a tree in *The Journals of Susanna Moodie*. In Jay Macpherson's *The Boatman* the fisherman-seeker is himself God's prey. So everyone is caught up in the world's ultimate mystery. Probably Birney's "Bushed," along with *The Double Hook* and *The Boatman*, contributes something to Atwood's later development of this theme.

The poet-novelists of recent times, enlarging upon the examples of native predecessors in the poetic or parabolic novel such as A.M. Klein and Sheila Watson and conscious of the usefulness to them of the methods of the twentieth-century symbolic novel, seek to depict in fiction rather than in epic verse a world of primal psychic conflict, a dark underground of the soul in which the horror that accompanies the world's glory insists on itself. This is found in *Beautiful Losers* (1966), in Ondaatje's *Collected Works of Billy the Kid* (1970) and *Coming through Slaughter* (1976), in David Helwig's *The Day before Tomorrow* (1971), in MacEwen's *King of Egypt, King of Dreams* (1971), and in Atwood's *Surfacing* (1972). In each case the vision of the author's already fairly substantial body of poetry is rendered more powerful and coherent, even though each of these novels is flawed. Each poet felt, apparently, that poetry, like patriotism, was not in itself enough.

Beautiful Losers may well have been the most influential of such recent works, but it was not the first. That honour goes to Douglas LePan's *The Deserter* (1964), a work that belongs unmistakably to the new climate of the 1960's even if it is an enlargement upon the themes and imagery of poems published in the late 1940's and early 1950's. With *Beautiful Losers*, it was a signal for new departures, and it repays a closer examination and appreciation than it has usually received. It has not enjoyed the popular success of *Beautiful Losers*, *Billy the Kid*, or *Surfacing*, but it belongs with them since it too is a highly evocative exploration of the necessary journey into the dark places of the psyche in order better to understand and to realize both self and an ideal of communion and community with others and the world.

LePan's version of this quest, dependent as was Klein's on the experience of an older generation, is informed by the shock and horror of the Second World War. Several of the author's early poems could serve as epigraphs, perhaps especially "One of the Regiment," whose soldier hero has burned his bridges behind him:

> No past, no future
> That he can imagine.

LePan's hero, Rusty, searches for lost perfection by going down into the dark, the night world of an anonymous city, modelled, quite obviously, on

London, which is seen as a lake of darkness or a drowned and wrecked Atlantis. At one point he dreams of Mycenaean bull-dancing. The Second World War has left him estranged from his ordinary past and unable to imagine a stable future.

In this work LePan paints a portrait of a world exhausted by war and depicts the brutal, squalid reality underlying the bourgeois hypocrisies, conventions, and pretences of industrialized Western life. At one point Rusty contemplates a large globe:

> He felt the world curving away beneath him like the side of someone dear, or someone sleeping. It was sleeping in exhaustion after a spasm that had affected city after city, country after country, desolating and ravaging and laying waste, had involved earth's farthest extremities, guano-islands lying far out to sea and veins of pitch-blende deep in the Arctic. It was sleeping, resting. But even in its sleep he could hear it heaving with undischarged torments, unsatisfied cravings. With dilated attention he was listening to the murmuring of millions of creatures who remembered being separated from the bough, who remembered falling like blossoms and then, it might be, being reunited to it in transient perfections (NCL, p. 183).

Rusty wants to find an order not based on brute force. Yet he wonders if the universe itself is not "only the long-continued rout after a cosmic disaster with the scattered remnants fleeing ever outwards" (p. 37). Thus the "big bang" theory of the origin of the expanding universe haunts many poets who long for some lost, perfect unity. Rusty wants to "retake paradise by storm, to re-enter it triumphantly; to recover the absolute he had tasted once before birth and then again in early adolescence and still a third time when his limbs had been mated to Althea's in annihilating surprise, completeness, joy" (p. 108). First and last things are stressed, as in Grove, Pratt, and many other Canadian writers. Rusty wanders in a drowned city and a wrecked cosmos; he is both (we are asked to believe) a simple, not particularly articulate hero of much physical and sexual prowess and a mystical seeker whose poetic consciousness is such that his ears "are sensitive to waves of all frequencies" so that "they brought him word of stars forming and bursting, of catastrophes taking place in other galaxies; they oscillated with continued high-pitched tinglings and cracklings. And he had no defences. The flood was alien and engulfing, and at such times he was powerless against it" (p. 108).

Many people would think that this was madness, or at least shell-shock. If so, it is the madness of that inchoate poet or mystic in all men who is still tuned-in to the cosmic frequencies, who has too much consciousness for ordinary survival. It is the full and dangerous awareness of both the glory and the horror of existence (the double hook); it is the swimmer's moment at the whirlpool (in Avison's version), which may, when accepted, lead to self-destruction or to a clearer vision of things, or to both; it is the madness of the grail-seeking knight at the Chapel Perilous.

On the second page of *The Deserter* Rusty is seen "looking into the sky as though it were the face of someone he had known, even of someone he had loved, but blank now, blank, he sometimes thought to himself, as though it had lost its reason" (p. 2). This is not only a general observation about the numbed state of the postwar world, but a kind of prophecy of the flawed glory of Anne, the schizophrenic woman Rusty eventually takes up with in the city. She is not his perfect memory, Althea (a goddess-figure, as her name suggests), though she has something of her quality. She is a creature of this present demented world. He is still in the army as he looks at the sky, but now he determines to desert, even though the war is over. He is a good soldier, and the army has constituted his order, but now he wants a better one. Part of his questioning may arise from the ironic sequence of events in which he has been decorated for conventional obedience to orders and then demoted as a consequence of a nonconformist act of true bravery. But it is the memory of Althea, a girl encountered briefly on leave in the city, that drives him on his quest. He is estranged from his family, despite his sister's excellent advice that no one is perfect. He is no longer the boy at home, and he is beginning to shed the identity given him by uniform and army. His "myriad selves" (p. 26) are to be set free. He has nothing, he feels, to lose, and must go. His is the problem of all young men—what to do with his life— but it is greatly exacerbated by the confused circumstances of the war and by his special sensitivity, that sense of the numinous—of the union of heaven and earth—which has transformed the encounter with Althea, who may, as he attempts to tell himself from time to time, have really been quite ordinary after all, into something quite magical. If it had not been her, he realizes, it would have been someone or something else that awakened his unappeasable longing. The horror of the war has helped to inspire a balancing sense of the paradisal in his consciousness. Seeking, he does not know just what he will find; he feels he is travelling under "sealed orders" (p. 21).

In the city Rusty wanders about in a sexual underworld of lonely, often pathetic human beings and their casual, sometimes brutal encounters. Seeking comfort from his friend Mark, who is a civil servant and part of the official "daytime" world, he is told that the war has given him a taste for extremity, that he is over-tempered (to use Milton Acorn's word) and must be cooled off or he will be dangerous to others. But he feels that his fury, his rage for perfection, comes from "further back" (p.50), from a desire for the original edenic wholeness before individual consciousness was split off from the great stem or golden bough of the universe. Mark replies that night-wandering is only half of experience, half of our consciousness, that he must live in the day-world of duty and social responsibility too. He says, "I know I'm split into two hemispheres, light and dark. I try to bind them together, though, so that I won't be destroyed" (p. 56). But Rusty is not ready for this notion of Jungian integration yet. He must go down into the dark before he can return to the light.

Rusty's sensitivity alienates him even from the other deserters, much as he may admire them. At a stag party where Rusty gets very drunk, hallucination (or vision) takes over. A somewhat unlikely conversation ensues, but the atmosphere is so vivid that it becomes poetic truth. The outlaws are seen as cavemen and animals; Rusty's consciousness travels backwards once again, entering a primitive world, the world of Plato's cave or Jung's collective unconscious. The beer keg in the centre of the room is "magnified by shadows until, resting on its wooden trestle, it seemed to lie at the heart of the celebration as though it were an animal—a young kid perhaps—steaming on an altar, or a bear to be disembowelled and eaten, every last scrap" (p. 153). Some primitive ritual is suggested:

Faces were slashed and scarified by black lines and chalk-white reflections, while above their heads stalked larger forms, shadows larger than life, furry or horned or antlered, crowning them, cresting them, almost brushing the ceiling. It might all have been a cave where primitive men had returned in triumph from the hunt and were now feasting in secure glee and defiance (p. 154).

The outlaws gathered here are seen as animals. Brandy (a bear) and Dragon (a stag) express and embody the amoral guiltless animal freedom and strength that Rusty admires but cannot quite accept. His longing for perfection separates him from them; he cannot agree with Brandy's insistence that nothing is perfect. He cannot forget Althea, and he insists that paradise exists, if only for the passing moment:

It exists. Freshened by dews...but then clouds over...disappears...a garden (you can build nothing there) and not a city...a garden that fades...fades; but leaves resplendent behind it unfading peacock dreams that feathering and fanning out on the roof of the cave, re-echoing greens and purples, have eyes to watch whether we will betray them. I am pierced. I dream of my dreams, watching the eyes that watch (p. 164).

Nothing can be built upon Rusty's experience of perfection, but it separates him from the other deserters forever. A higher moral consciousness is suggested in the image of the eyes that "watch whether we will betray them" from the top of the platonic cave of mind. Man has a responsibility to his best dreams, and Rusty must now look forward to some future Utopia, some impossible ideal city that combines order with the greatest possible degree of individual freedom and opportunity for self-realization.

In the latter chapters Rusty wonders whether his quest into darkness is not finished; it occurs to him that perhaps he should turn himself in. At the same time events build to a crisis with Steve, his friend, who is being intimidated by communist agents, with Anne, his mistress, who is approaching another breakdown, with a group of thugs who want his strength and co-operation in their activities, and with a mounting official campaign to round up deserters. He finds that he is, in spite of himself, involved in a kind of alternative society, involved in mankind, in community. One friend, one woman, and a group who pressure him are enough to make him once again a social being who is enmeshed in complicated problems and responsibilities. The underworld is shown to be, in some respects, a mirror-image of the official world. There are parallel meetings of police, embassy officials, and gangsters which are meant to seal the fate of Rusty and of the agent who pursues Steve. Rusty is now hunted down—from two directions. He is caught between two worlds and is fortunate to escape with his life. Earlier, Anne has left him for his own good as she feels her madness returning. In the hunt Steve is killed because Rusty leaves him alone, thinking he is safe. Rusty feels himself being followed; he feels that he himself is the battlefield or the city through which alternating bands of hunters and hunted move.

At this point the reader wonders whether Rusty's justifiable paranoia should not be allowed free rein. Should the book's atmosphere not become even more hallucinatory or Kafkaesque than it is? To achieve this degree of controlled hysteria LePan would probably have needed a first-person narration, Rusty's diary fragments or some such device to convey his immediate consciousness. The nightmarish quality of the hero's final wandering in the night might then have been heightened a good deal. On the other hand, perhaps the reader is supposed to admire Rusty's relative cool-headedness. He is not supposed to break down, like an ordinary mortal (like Steve, like Anne), but to come through into the light. And yet his pride is supposed at the end to have been "broken." Should he not then first go through a period of immersion in "madness" like that of the young woman in Atwood's *Surfacing*? Or was this inherent in the whole experience of wandering? There is here the hint of a technical problem, a problem of characterization, and I will return to it a little later.

As it is, Rusty survives and even triumphs, after a fashion. Desolate at the death of his friend Steve, which he feels is a result of his own "desertion," he contemplates suicide. But the remembered faith of Anne and Steve prevents him. He feels in himself, though now stripped even of honour, "a deep ultimate animal courage" (p. 294): this is the irreducible identity he has sought. He thinks a little later of Brandy and Dragon, finding relief and release from his sense of failure and misery in the realization of the "primitive and simple" energies that underlie whatever man may build: "in their animal heat was to be found conspicuously the final irreducible particles, random, unpredictable, not to be trusted, but without which nothing could be built, nothing, neither love nor justice nor a city, without which there could be no meaning nor anything but spreading tundra and despair" (p. 297). He feels the vision of perfection being broken within him, to be diffused in imperfect fragments, but not lost, always there as a dream that motivates imperfect individual man to move step by step towards the betterment of the conditions of existence for his fellows. He sees now that a community can, indeed *must* be built from our common sense of alienation from an imagined wholeness or perfection. And so he gives himself up and returns to society.

The Deserter is not a novel of character like *The Stone Angel*, which appeared in the same year, or of much outward event, though there is a great deal of psychological activity. It is carried by the highly evocative and sensuous language of solid, concrete description and of the suggestive metaphor and traditional myth. There is a close texture of recurrent images. Many of them are variations of what might be called the dominant image of twentieth-century art—fragmentation. Blossoms fall from a great bough in the sky, and the reader is led to imagine their impossible reunion. Rusty seeks Althea, an Aphrodite figure who unites heaven and the fecund sea, but becomes involved instead with Anne, a deteriorating psychotic who tells him, "your heart would have to break before you could give it to me" (p. 256). The world is a loved one who has gone mad; the peacock's tail with its myriad eyes represents fragments of a dream; a perfect crystal sun-dial, a microcosmic image of wholeness with the twelve signs of the zodiac on it, is shattered as the proud hero is brought to accept the necessary limitations of his human condition. He is finally better for being broken.

Other important imagery has to do with animals and the sword. Dragon and Brandy are seen as magnificent but irresponsible animals. Animal courage must, somehow, be made to serve civilization. This theme explains LePan's recurrent references to heraldic (that is, civilized, leashed, tethered) bears, stags, leopards and, most civilized of all and suggestive of Rusty's aspiration, unicorns. The unicorn is special, and his horn symbolic of creative rather than destructive power. Rusty himself is not presented as a particular animal, though—as Dragon and Brandy are—but as a sword that is being tested. It is a sword that will not be new to readers of LePan's poems; they will recall the "strict and healing blade" of love ("The Wounded Prince"), and, more appropriately, Excalibur, the magic weapon of King Arthur, which expresses a temperament both sensitive and strong ("A Fallen Prophet"). In *The Deserter* the sword metaphor is employed to suggest Rusty's task as a warrior, his phallic animal nature, and his eventual role as the refined weapon or instrument of civilization. He is too sensitive to be an outlaw; he is rather "a roving picket" who goes down into the dark "to find out where we are and what has gone wrong" (p. 192).

Rusty's confused questing seems to be for an order more complete and perfect than that devised by human society, an order not finally based on brute force. He seeks the perfect realization of both his animal instincts and his vague otherworldly aspirations outside society, journeying at once into the underworld of the novel's anonymous city and into the dark part of his own nature. What he learns is that human society, however imperfect and however unfriendly to the free individual, is better than the chaos it holds at bay. He discovers further that the perfection he seeks is impossible and that the animal freedom of the outlaw is not a personal solution to his problem since it is a temperamental impossibility for him, however much he may admire it in others. He is not able really to desert society; inevitably the path leads back.

There is often a strong element of romance in the Canadian novel, even at its most realistic, as any very careful examination of the work of Morley Callaghan, Hugh MacLennan, Ernest Buckler and others reveals. Here, though, it seems to be paramount, as it is in *The Second Scroll*. LePan presents a modern version of the quest-romance, one somewhat easier to follow than *The Waste Land*. But the very attempt to make the work rich and yet easily comprehensible can make for difficulties. The novel proceeds both by a literal progression of events and by a poetic evocation of Rusty's developing awareness. There is a curious and sometimes rather jarring movement back and forth between quite straightforward narrative and poetic splendour.

LePan has written of what he regards as a natural tendency for some Canadian writers, the attempt to write "in terms of what happens in an anonymous setting to an anonymous, or virtually anonymous, hero" in order to create "a work of almost universal luminosity which can be understood anywhere."[2] This is at the other pole, obviously, from LePan's own explicitly "Canadian" poems, and from the tradition of the Canadian regional novel; but such a novel as *The Mountain and the Valley* also aims at universality, the universal in the particular, and it can certainly be seen as a romance or fable, the account of a quest that fails. Now *The Deserter* is

set in an anonymous capital—though it is recognizably London, rather than
New York or Montreal or Rome or some other "fabled city" that might
interest a Klein or a Callaghan. And Rusty is too anonymous in the sense
that he is at once too simply the physical "hero" and yet too sensitive to
human and cosmic vibrations to be anything but a representative or mythic
figure. He is a little like MacLennan's Jerome Martell in these respects. He
is gold-crusted, heroic in the old sense, and this is acceptable. The
misgivings arise when the literal is presented too flatly or there is insistence
on how ordinary Rusty is. LePan seems to be suggesting, admirably
enough, that inchoate visions come to ordinary men too, especially in
wartime. He seems to want to be democratic and aristocratic at once. But
the mundane and the heroic planes are not always so beautifully fused into a
single prose-poem as in the brilliant opening chapter.

This problem might have been solved or avoided by the use of what—in
relation to such romances as *Moby Dick, Heart of Darkness, The Great
Gatsby, The Second Scroll,* and *The Watch That Ends the Night*—might be
called the dual protagonist. In each of these works a narrator comments
upon the often tragic experience of another man and is brought to new
maturity or insight in the process of this "secret sharing." It is the effect of
Ahab on Ishmael, Kurtz on Marlowe, Gatsby on Carraway, Jerome
Martell on George Stewart, and Melech on the narrator of *The Second
Scroll* that is important. In this case, the narrator—the Marlowe or
Ishmael—would have to be Mark, a character who resembles his creator in
certain obvious ways and who regards Rusty as an alter ego. The principle
here is that if Ishmael or Carraway are believable, then it is easier to accept on
faith the somewhat preposterous pseudo-Shakespearian tragic hero Ahab
and the almost equally preposterous arch-romantic Gatsby. The bizarre is
made credible by the narrative voice of Marlowe or Carraway or good, safe,
old George Stewart. It is an excellent way to involve the reader or to lead him
gently, as MacLennan puts it, into experience whose intensity and terror he
might otherwise wish to avoid.

However, if Mark were the narrator of *The Deserter* and were playing the
role of commentator like Marlowe or George Stewart, he would
presumably have to confine his flights of poetry to key moments in the
narrative. The work would lose much of the intense, heightened, excessive
language which is the most striking—and for those with a taste for the
baroque and for writers who still have the nerve to go for baroque—the
most attractive feature of *The Deserter.* It is preferable to have the work as
it is, even if anyone as heroic as Rusty is not believable, or at least not when
he is found in a modern setting. But after all Ahab is not really believable as
a human being either, despite the persuasiveness of Ishmael's controlling
voice. In any case, literature would be poorer without the rich experience of

Moby Dick, that overlong, clumsy, uneven monster of a book; and the gorgeous excesses of *The Deserter*, which has an equally significant and indeed somewhat similar theme, should not be missed either.

LePan is the first notable Canadian poet-novelist of the 1960's. Because of his concern for "universal luminosity," his development of the interrelated themes of community, achievement of wholeness and identity, and the role of the "primitive" in these avoids any reference to Canada. But his "myth" of duality, fragmentation and a possible reintegration of self and community is consistent with those of the younger poet-novelists who do write overtly of Canada, particularly with *Beautiful Losers* which is also concerned with light and dark, spirit and senses, insanity and vision, goddesses and primitive power, and with *Surfacing*, in which the notion of a self and a country trapped under water, unrealized but potential, is implicit.

Notes

1. See Leslie Monkman's "Coyote as Trickster in *The Double Hook*," *Canadian Literature* 52 (1972), and Philip Child's "A Canadian Prose-Poem," *Dalhousie Review* 39 (1959).
2. "The Dilemma of the Canadian Author," *Atlantic Monthly*, November 1964.

A History of Us All

Leonard Cohen

Leonard Cohen is probably now the most famous of Canadian writers. This is because he has become a popular songwriter and performer, thus resolving (for himself at any rate) the dilemma of his predecessor A.M. Klein and moving a step beyond his older friend Irving Layton towards public success. It seems a good idea, though, to ignore the public image once beloved of the young—lugubrious Leonard, the mournful troubadour—and to concentrate on the work. In 1955 Hugh MacLennan wrote to the romantic young man whom he had encountered at McGill: "You have the two rare gifts of rhythm and naked feeling and as you know, the latter is both painful and priceless."[1] It was a perceptive observation. The young man was already writing accomplished lyric poems of an escapist and self-absorbed kind. These are suffused with the imagery of the Old Testament, as would be expected, but also with Christianity, since Cohen, like a good Canadian, like the Klein of *The Rocking Chair*, wanted to compare mythologies, and with the idea of giving and receiving pain. Sado-masochism was an important ingredient in his work from the beginning.

The poems are full of mythology and fairy tales. In the first novel, *The Favourite Game*, the references to Mary Poppins and to Peter Pan, the boy who refused to grow up, are highly appropriate to the situation of the "hero." Elsewhere the worlds of sleep, dream, madness, romance, or impersonal orgiastic sex are invoked in poems like "You Have the Lovers," "Two Went to Sleep," "Story," and "Now of Sleeping." These are, of course, *adult* fairy tales, that is, kinky. Cohen does not write for actual children, as those somewhat kinkier and infinitely more repressed Victorians and Edwardians—Lewis Carroll, Edward Lear, Oscar Wilde, J.M. Barrie, and others—did. They could hide behind the false but imposing stability of their age, escaping from it in their "children's" art. But Cohen is a "decadent" writer of the atomic age, a time in which many feel like helpless, sexually anarchic, and politically impotent children much of the time. The popular songs, like some of the early poems and like *Beautiful Losers*, deal in salvation through degradation in a world of masters and victims. This can easily be parodied (for example, "there are heroes in the garbage"), but it obviously speaks to a great many people, especially the confused and frustrated young who are always the least, not the most, liberated members of any society.

Klein and Layton are decidedly not "black" romantics of this kind.[2] Layton believes in the flesh but not in degradation or masochism. Still, Cohen has been influenced by his predecessors in Montreal. Klein has written charming rhymes for children and simple love poems, and some of Cohen's simpler and more straight lyrics ("Go by Brooks," "As the Mist Leaves No Scar") may reflect that influence. The early Cohen's customary delicacy and quietness of tone are, in any case, closer to some of Klein's work than to Layton's. When Cohen writes his version of "The Cold Green Element" and calls it "If it were spring," he is at once less strident and more morbid than Layton. He speaks of killing a man, hanging him from a tree, and turning him into art as a "mercy." Is death, is murder the necessary condition of "art" for him? Must this world be annihilated, as Edgar Allan Poe seemed to want to do? When he writes his version of Layton's "Cain" it is terse and pointed, a minor masterpiece:

> A moth drowned in my urine,
> his powdered body finally satin.
> My eyes gleamed in the porcelain
> like tiny dancing crematoria.
>
> History is on my side, I pleaded,
> as the drain drew circles in his wings.
> (Had he not been bathed in urine
> I'd have rescued him to dry in the wind.)
>
> "Inquiry into the Nature of Cruelty"

Man is cruel out of aesthetic distaste for the world's ugliness and out of a fascination with pain, he suggests. His excuse—after the fact—is the excuse of the Nazis for the treatment of those they consigned to their "crematoria": that history, or evolution, is on his side.

In some of his love poems and some of his songs Cohen specializes in goodbyes. The speaker glories in leaving love behind, in being solitary, in having only transient loves, in making his emotion and the love object herself perfect and impersonal by terminating the affair. Once again love, life, is only the raw material for art: narcissism and emotional masturbation triumph. This is, of course, the psychology of Lawrence Breavman in Cohen's first novel, *The Favourite Game*. It is a popular fantasy with wide appeal to men and women, as Bliss Carman also knew: the romantic wanderer, eternally restless, always a stranger everywhere he goes, leaving his magic touch on many lovers. It is, as Michael Ondaatje has observed in his book on Cohen, the lover and not the beloved who is glorified in this myth. Indeed, Lawrence Breavman would seem to be a case of terminal narcissism—almost wholly egocentric and unsympathetic if it were not for his and his creator's saving graces: wit, irony, and a marvellous gift for aphorism. These make the early novel quite readable, even though it fails to achieve the objectivity of *Beautiful Losers* and is a good deal less interesting.

Irony seems to have been the only relief for Breavman's oppressive self-enclosure. In his poems, however, Cohen makes a valiant attempt to go beyond solipsism to public concerns in *Flowers for Hitler*. The intention is admirable even though much of the poetry is awful. It is an interesting transitional book in which Cohen reaches for a tougher, sparer idiom, as he does once again in *The Energy of Slaves*, an equally uneven and ultimately unsuccessful attempt to get beyond romantic self-absorption. The theme that dominates *Flowers* is collective human guilt for the atrocities of our time, and this is interesting, but there is much gratuitous cleverness and expansive public posing. On the other hand there is a very finely crafted poem, "For E.J.P.," apparently precipitated by the death of Pratt in 1964 though E.L.P., Ezra Pound, would have been a more suitable dedicatee, in which the poet appears to abandon aestheticism; in the equally successful "Style" he promises to forget his old style.

Subsequently, he has written songs. A few of these are equally good as poems: "Suzanne" is the best and most famous example. Such poems may be the simplest, most perfect, and most readily communicable that exist. The songs of Shakespeare and Ben Jonson, the songs of Robert Burns, and W.B. Yeats's "Song of Wandering Aengus," which is sung by Judy Collins, are poems of this kind. No great emotional or intellectual complexity is likely in such poems, but they are immediately pleasing and very durable.

However, Cohen's earliest poems—those of *Let Us Compare Mythologies* and *The Spice-Box of Earth*—are his best. An early poem such as "Summer Night," which describes an encounter with the Canadian space, is a far more accomplished public statement than any of the later fragments or ramblings in which the poet appears to be influenced detrimentally by the American Beats. Thereafter, he grew as a novelist while he declined as a poet; most of his songs do not have the interest of "Suzanne" when they are read on the page. Indeed, it once seemed possible that Cohen could develop into a significant novelist. Unfortunately, the rather self-indulgent and repetitive prose poems of *Death of a Lady's Man*, his most recent book, suggest that he is unlikely to do so.

Meanwhile, there is *Beautiful Losers*, a work that has not been easy to come to terms with at first encounter. Critics have even found more or less opposite messages in it. In *Savage Fields*, for example, Dennis Lee attempts to pin Cohen down and is frustrated by his speculative playfulness. Such confusion arises from Cohen's ambivalence, his detachment, his tendency to play with ideas and human possibilities without finally committing himself to them. There is not here the earnestness of LePan, MacEwen, or Atwood. Cohen is not endorsing anything; he is exploring certain human possibilities. He has warned us himself that his art is never wholly devoid of "the con," and this presumably means conjuring as well as confidence tricks.

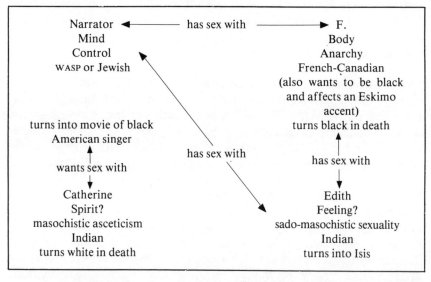

Beautiful Losers has four important characters: a narrator; his lifelong friend and lover F.; his late wife Edith, a member of the Indian tribe of "A—s," who was also F.'s lover; and Catherine Tekakwitha (1656-1680), an Indian "saint" studied by the narrator, who wants a sexual union with her. The relations of these four are recounted by the narrator and then by F., after which there is an epilogue in the third person: these offer different perspectives on the bizarre and passionate experience of all four. Catherine and Edith are both Indians, though their experiences are at opposite poles of asceticism (or masochism) and total sensuality, respectively. They balance each other in an extreme way, and perhaps blend into one another as extreme pleasure becomes pain and vice versa. F. is an extreme sensualist and Québécois revolutionary whose initial can stand for Friend, French, Fuck, Fantasy, Frankenstein, Flesh, Feeling, Fraud, and perhaps a number of other things, while the narrator is a physically and emotionally constipated scholar who might, conveniently, be either Jewish or WASP, or both. It has frequently been suggested that F. and the narrator are aspects of one person. No doubt all four characters are aspects of one person, or country, whose fantasy the novel is, whose plea seems to be "Put me together." But they are also distinct within it, at least until the last section.

Let us look at the four characters as a quaternity. Is the crazy constellation of sexes and races and metamorphoses Canada herself? Certainly there is a vision of Canada's history and present situation as well as an eclectic mixture of Indian, Christian, American pop, and Greek mythologies, not to mention Isis, the Universal Mother, who is identified with Edith, who may then be seen as a kind of Althea, a "holy star." "Is it," says the narrator, "because I've stumbled on the truth about Canada? I don't want to stumble on the truth about Canada" (Bantam, p. 43). And later to F.: "You've turned Canada into a vast analyst's couch from which we dream and re-dream nightmares of identity" (p. 169).

(I am reminded by all of this of an encounter with Irving Layton on the first evening of the Klein Symposium at the University of Ottawa in 1974. He said in his playful fashion, "You're looking very Slavic these days!" I replied that I was Scottish, English, Irish, French and Norwegian, and that's all as far as I knew. "But I'd like to have some Jewish and some Indian too, to be more completely Canadian," or words to that effect. "Tom," said Irving, "you mustn't be racially greedy.")

Part One of *Beautiful Losers*, "The History of Them All," is the narrator's account of his wife and friend and his obsession with Catherine Tekakwitha and the A—s, the tribe of losers and failures that he studies and with whom he identifies. It is later made clear that all human beings—even Hitler—are A—s in need of comfort from Isis. But Edith has committed suicide as Part One begins, and F. attempts to rescue the narrator from his own pedantry. He tells him the Indians were like ancient Greeks and that they had their own acropolis, which was painted red, but the narrator cannot appreciate the imaginative truth of this fantasy. Edith—who was F.'s creation, a beautiful woman made out of an Indian girl with acne—had also attempted to restore a primitive Dionysian fire to hers and her husband's lives by painting herself red and asking him to do the same, but he had made her wash it off. Perhaps Edith had wanted to regain her former imperfect but authentic red self again.

F. tells the narrator to "connect nothing" (despite the connections he himself makes), because his academic connections would be "pathetic." He tells him further that their sex is not strictly homosexual because F. was once a girl. The narrator protests that he knows this is not true, and F. remarks disdainfully, "Thus do the starving refuse sustenance" (p. 23). He seems to be speaking here of the androgynous nature of the human psyche, as Robertson Davies does more obliquely in *Fifth Business*, another novel concerned, but in a more distanced and infinitely less poetic manner, with saints and magic, but the narrator misses the point.

F. preaches the total eroticizing of the body à la Norman O. Brown. "Down with genital imperialism! All flesh can come!" (p. 40). Sex becomes "ordinary eternal machinery" (p. 41), and political revolution is seen to be sexually stimulating as a separatist rally becomes an orgy, for the narrator, at least. But he finds F.'s and Edith's erotic revolution alien to him for the most part. And Catherine Tekakwitha rejected her sexuality very early, giving herself over to another extreme, to the alien Christian culture. Thus her reward is to turn white in death, like D.C. Scott's equally unfortunate Keejigo. Her life was a mortification of the flesh: her savage intensity is dedicated to an extreme masochism. In a parallel passage we learn that Edith had been raped as a teen-ager "in a stone quarry or an abandoned mine, someplace very mineral and hard, owned indirectly by U.S. interests" (p. 75), that is, she is victimized as the Indians and then Quebec have been victimized. F. holds the theory that "White America has been punished by lung cancer for having destroyed the Red Man and stolen his pleasures" (p. 113). He resorts to extreme measures—such as the drive to Ottawa with its faked car-crash—to recover the "Indian" or "Greek" magic, the "energy of love" (p. 121) that the saint rides. Perhaps then F. is going to sensational extremes to right the balance, to balance the other extreme explored by Catherine Tekakwitha and associated with Christianity. Cohen's song "Suzanne" seems to express such a balance. It is interesting in this regard that the story in which Catherine Tekakwitha's spilled wine turns the frozen white world red is told by Edith after she and F. have been shooting up with holy water. Each wishes to recover the dark and the primitive that Catherine attempted to leave behind.

But extremes meet, and both lead to self-destruction. Edith commits suicide after telling the story of Catherine's Feast, and Catherine's religious life is a long suicide. F. drives himself to the madness of syphilis as he attempts to represent and be a self-sacrificial saint for all minorities and outcasts— blacks, Québécois, Indians, homosexuals, junkies, orphans, and so forth. In his letter from the hospital F. attempts to explain himself: he feared rationality and wanted to drive his pupil a little mad. He foresaw the "New Jew" who "loses his mind gracefully," who overthrows old prejudices and stigmas and is "the founder of Magic Canada, Magic French Quebec, and Magic America" (p. 203). He confounds all systems and beliefs because these are tyranny. "He dissolves history and ritual by accepting unconditionally the complete heritage" (p. 203). The New Jew—Cohen himself?—restores magic by mixing mythologies and eliminating or transcending history (the "System Theatre"). Yet only the narrator is to accomplish this; Edith and F. are left drained after their sado-masochistic orgy with the Danish Vibrator and Hitler in Argentina. F. realizes that there are limits to his ability to manipulate others and sees that Edith, whether Indian orphan with acne or his beautiful creation, is ultimately beyond him, is Isis or all women. F.'s own "system" fails too. He has tried to be a magician when he should have been magic; that is, he should have surrendered himself to the "energy of love."

F.'s politics are expressed as follows:

> The English did to us what we did to the Indians, and the Americans did to the English what the English did to us. I demanded revenge for everyone. I saw cities burning, I saw movies falling into blackness. I saw the maize on fire. I saw the Jesuits punished. I saw the trees taking back the long-house roofs. I saw the shy deer murdering to get their dresses back. I saw the Indians punished. I saw chaos eat the gold roof of parliament. I saw water dissolve the hoofs of drinking animals. I saw the bonfires covered with urine, and the gas stations swallowed up entire, highway after highway falling into the wild swamps (pp. 236-37).

F. demands universal revenge. Klein's awareness of the historical fate of Indians and Québécois is here extended and intensified to include English-Canadians and those victims of all groups of men: plants and animals. History, not to mention evolution, is a tale of continuous injustice, a matter of Jews and Nazis moving from one role to the other, an endless affair of torturers and victims caught up in machinery and system of one kind or another. F.'s proposed solution seems unlikely of realization. Indeed, the temptation to take his proposals of liberation wholly seriously is undercut by the comic tone and incident of most episodes and by the realization of his and Edith's fates, as well as by the ambiguous apotheosis of the narrator, the smelly old man who is supposed to accomplish the human liberation from history, in Part III.

The narrator has been living for years in F.'s treehouse, suffering like St. Simeon Stylites. But one spring day, pursued by police, he leaves. He has given up eating (except for some obliging cunnilingus with an Isis-figure who gives him a lift), like saints of the past, and his eyes blink so quickly that he has, for himself, abolished the film in the System Theatre. He has transcended history. Finally he becomes a movie of Ray Charles, the soul of whose art transcends its materials, which are the sufferings under historical injustice of American blacks. He appears to have triumphed as he disappears into the sky or the "machine," perhaps, since the New Jew abolishes system by accepting everything. He gives himself up to the universe, and presumably becomes a saint.

The novel then concludes with a request from the Jesuits for the beatification of Catherine Tekakwitha, and then a very personal statement of welcome, apparently to the reader, who is addressed as a lover, as indeed he is if he enters the anarchic and polymorphously erotic world of F. and the New Jew.

But it would be dangerous to assume that Cohen is doing more than playing with these ideas. The book is playful and speculative and ironic and uneven throughout. The narrator has a healthy Canadian suspicion of all this "guru shit," and so—in some moods—does Guru Cohen. Later remarks in *The Energy of Slaves* seem to bear this out. The "message" of such a novel as this is surely that there can be no consistent or complete or final message: a "Zen Ph.D." is "tolerated" (p. 174). Ray Charles's art, or Cohen's, may transcend its historical materials, but it does not alter the facts of history or of our contemporary situation. Canada remains a crazy quilt created by historical conflicts that continue in a variety of psychological forms. The liberation of art occurs, but in another dimension. Still, it helps us to live more consciously in the present one. Cohen has no programmatic solution for the problems he poses; instead he offers a greater awareness of their nature and of the perverse nature of a confused world so that men may continue to live in it. The utopian proposals of Norman O. Brown are treated with irony and transformed into humour—they remain proposals only in Cohen's ambivalent use of them. He is not a definitive teacher, he is an artist who "wanders" in his time, as he says in a song, seeking "a kind of balance." Still, he is not a wandering sceptic like Birney; he believes in God and does not know what God purposes.

Beautiful Losers yields up fascinating insights into the nature of Canada and of modern confused man. And it is often very entertaining. But some of the pop or automatic writing is tedious; some of the comic devices do not work. It is, however, easier to read than the work of William Burroughs, which was probably one formal influence—Thomas Pynchon's *V* may be another. Cohen's talent for witty aphorism, here sometimes transformed into parody, stands him in good stead. The novel remains an achievement that is more, somehow, than the sum of its uneven parts. It opened the door to serious experimental fiction in Canada. Like *The Deserter*, it offers another angle on chaos, and it remains the most remarkable achievement of one of Canada's most extraordinary and uneven poets.

Notes

1. Quoted in Tony Kilgallin, "The Beaver and the Elephant," *TLS*, 26 October 1973.
2. See Sandra Djwa's "Leonard Cohen, Black Romantic," *Canadian Literature* 34 (1967).

Deeper Darkness,
after Choreography

Michael Ondaatje

If LePan's and Cohen's myths have to do with an expedition or descent into darkness, horror, a mystical sensuality, fragmentation, and madness, then Michael Ondaatje's work could be said to carry this movement to a further, darker extreme. For here there is virtually no intimation of the possibility of return or reintegration, of transcendence or the possible achievement of community (or even a more than momentary communication), at least for the author's doomed heroes. Ondaatje's is, thus far, a darker and apparently more nihilistic vision than those of Watson, Klein, LePan, Cohen, MacEwen, Atwood, or Helwig, in whose work more positive human possibilities still exist even in the midst of darkness.

This is a development from Cohen, if not exactly progress. Dennis Lee, who chooses in *Savage Fields* to discuss Ondaatje *before* Cohen, for his own reasons, even goes so far as to assert, somewhat arbitrarily, that the nihilistic world-consciousness of *Billy the Kid*, a book Lee himself edited, is today "in the ascendant." And certainly the Ondaatje hero's destiny, as exemplified in strong poems like "Peter" and "White Dwarfs," in the quasi-novel in prose and poetry, *Billy the Kid*, and in *Coming through Slaughter*, seems to be to move further and further from social and purposeful being. In this respect his vision seems rather more American than Canadian, and his choices of American historical-legendary protagonists such as William Bonney and Buddy Bolden are appropriate to the demands of this myth.

It is, no doubt, of significance here that Ondaatje is not a native Canadian. Though he began to develop his extraordinary gift after his arrival in the new world, his earliest and most profound emotions and intuitions were shaped elsewhere, in far-off Sri Lanka. But he has been familiar with much of the best Canadian writing throughout his early career and has adapted the tradition to his own ends. Both Pratt's narratives of violence and Cohen's fragmented narrative have influenced him.

Early reviewers were correct in recognizing Ondaatje's markedly individual if eccentric talent. An obsession with violence has also contributed to his popularity in these apocalyptic times. Whence this comes remains a mystery, though it is something that he shares with Pratt and Cohen, among other Canadian writers. His interest in animals is a thing common in Canada, too, of course: but his animals seem to be descendants of Ted Hughes's animals, who are in turn descendants of D.H. Lawrence's animals. And the exoticism of treatment, while it has an obvious kinship with that of Wallace Stevens, whom Ondaatje introduces to King Kong, is presumably Ceylonese in origin. By means of these interests, the poems attempt to reveal the wonder, beauty, and horror of an inner life on which "civilized" society tries to keep the lid very tightly clamped. This is his version of the notorious Canadian garrison-and-wilderness theme. All in all, a heady mixture: the general effect is strange and intriguing to Canadians, and quite rightly. Both what speaks to traditional concerns and what is new has an appeal. The variety and the meeting of many traditions gives the country somewhat variable cultural possibilities and thus a soul capable of growth, rather than a rigidly defined role-playing social or national ego.

Ondaatje is at his best in longer works. In the longish poems "Paris" and "Peter," which is a kind of portrait of the artist as persecuted and misunderstood monster, his characteristic extravagance is subordinated to the overall theme in a satisfying way. Ondaatje seeks out the heroic in the mythic past, as Gwendolyn MacEwen does; "Paris" has the same magic as her "Arcana" series. A longer sequence, *The Man With Seven Toes*, is striking as well. It concerns a woman lost in the Australian bush, and this situation is at least analogous to the encounter with Canada's very different nature. It is purer than the earlier narratives, in a sense; it cannot be construed as allegory or disguised autobiography as they could. Ondaatje's descriptions of violent events have a tactile and kinetic quality that is somewhat rare in poetry, and the absence of any meditation or apparent moral or other attitude to his materials gives the work startling immediacy and power. But it is with *Billy the Kid* that he finds a vehicle, albeit an American one, large enough for the fuller expression of his vision.

Reading this extraordinary work, one suspects at first that Ondaatje relishes the bizarre or the whimsical or the grotesque for its own sake; but a little reflection makes it apparent that this is how he wants the reader, at least temporarily, to perceive the world. The true story of the historical William Bonney is not all that important here, in spite of what certain, perhaps stunned, reviewers have written. He is irrecoverable, anyhow, as

Ondaatje's stress on the slipperiness of legend and of reality itself makes clear. Beneath the world's apparent order, beneath all civilized decorum, is a mindless ferocity. By implication, the reader is asked to prefer the "natural" (that is, animal, even cosmic) murderousness of Billy to the efficient killing of the near-mechanical "sane assassin" Pat Garrett, but in any case the world itself appears to be insane or at least very delicately balanced:

> The beautiful machines pivoting on themselves
> sealing and fusing to others
> and men throwing levers like coins at them.
> And there is there the same stress as with stars,
> the one altered move that will make them maniac.

Garrett wants to understand and analyse everything and everyone: he is an "academic" killer, a critic perhaps. Billy, by way of contrast, has a poet's imagination that Garrett perceives as "usually pointless and never in control" (p. 43); but even Garrett sees him as an artist with superhuman faculties that "civilized" man has lost. It is difficult to "admire" Billy, as even his appointed assassin Garrett does, but Ondaatje did provide another view. Eventually Billy's friend Sallie Chisum concludes, "Billy was a fool" in the uncollected Ondaatje poem "Sallie Chisum, Last Words, 4 a.m." The contrasted killers represent, perhaps, two sides of Ondaatje the poet or of man.

The book seems to suggest that Billy is more sinned against (by authorities anxious for "progress") than sinning, but nothing finally is certain except that both his faults and his virtues are human and representative, though much magnified. Legend and reality blend. The brilliantly fragmented narrative involves both poetry and prose, the latter much more vital and evocative, flashforwards and flashbacks, a comic book about Billy, references to Ondaatje's friends such as Captain Poetry or b.p. nichol, recorded statements from those who actually knew Bonney, genuine period photos and one that purports to be John and Sallie Chisum but is in fact Kingston poet Stuart MacKinnon and his wife Sally, a Bonney girlfriend named Angie Dickinson (signalling the author's admiration for a certain film star), a bizarre story of mad dogs deliberately inbred (not likely the result of historical research), a photo of Michael O. as a small boy in Ceylon dressed in a cowboy outfit: different perspectives on ultimately mysterious experience. A fascinating world, a colourful but horrifying universe is thus created: it is an inferno of literal heat and drought, of violence and madness relieved only by brief moments of humour or of peace and beauty, most of these focused on the Chisum ranch, a kind of oasis in the general desert of horror. God either is dead or is the force that visits upon Billy his horrific poet's vision of wounds in the air. He believes he is mind-fucked by "Jesus." It is a world untouched by any sense of hope (such as that felt in the work of the Christian rationalist and optimist Pratt, who was also obsessed with elemental violence) or by any developed moral sense more complicated than "love your friends and kill your enemies." That is, I suppose, a large part of its appeal. Ondaatje seeks the "mythic" in all its primitive horror, as Gwendolyn MacEwen sometimes has done. The aesthetic effect of violence in itself interests him. He looks for odd angles and perspectives like the director of an avant garde western movie.

Is this escapist, atavistic, an evasion of the moral complexity of "civilization"? I think the author might say: this is the way things are, under the surface. Deep within we can respond to this and even in our ambivalence secretly desire it. Canadians, who can know elemental ferocity just as well as Ceylonese or ancient Greeks, do respond to Ondaatje's world, whether they are prepared wholly to assent to so bleak a view of things or not. In *Savage Fields* Dennis Lee says that "world" or "consciousness-dominated planet" is at internecine war with "earth" or "instinctually driven planet" in *Billy the Kid* and in our lives. This is surely not the whole truth about the world or about human life, but it is nevertheless a tremendous vision, with its own integrity, and *The Collected Works of Billy the Kid* a very fine, powerful, and challenging book.

Rat Jelly is a collection of individual poems, and thus it is related more to *The Dainty Monsters* than to the books in-between. It is an advance on that book, which was uneven. It contains poems of "loathing" (for all except family, friends and heroes—his own island), domestic poems (in which the domestic tends to the legendary), poems about the artist as spider, a powerful poem about the poet's father, poems about animals, and a final poem about the void, the silence underneath, within and beyond all relationship, brotherhood, love—the stunning "White Dwarfs." The logic of the attitudes expressed here suggests a movement to silence, to the place where speech is meaningless. It is a black or negative mysticism, or perhaps a dark night of the soul. But Ondaatje is too much in love with "choreography," with bright colours, images and sounds, with the erotic force in the world, to give it all up at this point. He has developed his own original and flexible free-verse style in which language is often pared down, all unnecessary words, especially articles, eliminated, in order to render the movement of the moment "to the clear." There is more for him to say—more about people and their relationships, more about human society.

Coming through Slaughter, Ondaatje's first novel proper, is, however, a kind of enlargement upon the theme of "White Dwarfs." Once again the author insists upon an art that culminates in silence and darkness. The book, an arrangement of brief and vividly effective prose passages interspersed with pieces of poetry here and there, is somewhat more perfectly executed and balanced than *Billy the Kid*, which had its ragged edges and its quirky or less interesting parts, but it is also rather less challenging, perhaps because readers have become acclimatized to Ondaatje's artist-(or hero)-in-deeper-and-deeper-isolation theme. This time the ambience is New Orleans, wonderfully evoked or invented, and the hero, jazzman Buddy Bolden, who was never recorded and who went mad: two circumstances that, I suspect, appeal greatly to the author. Bolden's art and inner experience are lost, but he may have encountered chaos purely before retiring into silence. His mind, Ondaatje writes, is "helpless against every moment's headline" (Anansi, p. 15). He does "nothing but leap into the mass of changes and explore them and all the tiny facets" (p. 15). Themes of friendship, love, and sexual jealousy are subordinate to this basic theme: "he was tormented by order, what was outside it" (p. 37).

The apparent impossibility of finding a wholly adequate form for the apparently formless: this is a problem no serious artist can escape. Like Atwood, Ondaatje makes frequent use of and reference to photography as one way of expressing this theme. The grotesque photographer Bellocq is Buddy's foil, a voyeur-artist who takes pictures of whores and then slashes the prints for satisfaction, his interior journey more obviously bizarre than Bolden's own. His perfect isolation, which culminates in suicide, fascinates Buddy. "They had talked for hours moving gradually off the edge of the social world. As Bellocq lived at the edge in any case he was at ease there and as Buddy did not he moved on past him like a naive explorer looking for footholds" (p. 64).

There are no prizes, Ondaatje concludes, for such exploration. This is a less violent fable, though there is violence, than the earlier ones in poetry and prose, but it is meant to disturb. The question that arises is whether it is really necessary for a fictional artist to *pursue* (as opposed to perceiving and experiencing without succumbing to) void or chaos to this suicidal extent. Perhaps, imaginatively, it is necessary, if only as a caution to others, including the fairly successful and prize-winning Michael Ondaatje himself. He can ride chaos, if his heroes cannot. Is it not possible, though, that there is something just a bit sentimental about this latest highly coloured version of the myth of the exemplary doomed hero or "beautiful" loser? Is there not a whole social world of more immediate and potentially fascinating human problems that is equally the artist's province and rather more profitable a field for Ondaatje (or, for that matter, Cohen) the novelist in future, if he is not to begin repeating himself in less and less rewarding ways? It is one of the paradoxes of this novel that Ondaatje *does* begin to explore a social world of complex human relationships even as he pursues his obsessive interest in the man beyond "social fuel." *Coming through Slaughter* is, in any case, his most accomplished performance to date.

Like Watson, LePan, Cohen, MacEwen, and Atwood, Ondaatje attempts in his parables to reveal an ultimate darkness, violence, chaos, flux, mystery; unlike them, he has little so far, beyond the common sense of Sallie Chisum's last words, to suggest about how one might live in the face of this.

Arcana Canadiana

Gwendolyn MacEwen

In some ways a female counterpart of Cohen and Ondaatje, Gwendolyn MacEwen can certainly be seen to share some of their concerns. Like them, she builds upon the Canadian tradition that went before. But she is more a celebrant than either.

MacEwen is a singer: her urgent and exuberant utterance creates a strong impression even when, as in many of the early poems, it approaches incoherency. A love of sheer sound, encouraged by her early poetic idols, Hart Crane and Dylan Thomas, can run away with the poem. In her work from the beginning there is a fascination with other times and worlds (as in Cohen and Ondaatje) but also a passionate longing for the integration of opposites or pairs—light and dark, male and female, past and future (as in *Beautiful Losers*). Hers too is the alchemical search for the divine in the mundane; magic and myth abound, and, again as in Cohen or Ondaatje, they are usually dramatized far more effectively, in terms of human action and a colloquial, flexible voice, than in the more traditional lyrics of Jay Macpherson or Eli Mandel.

MacEwen is also aware that the cosmos she explores is finally herself:

By eating the world you may enclose it.

seek simplicities; the fingerprints of the sun only
and the fingernail of the moon duplicating you in
 your body,
the cosmos fits your measure; has no ending.

"The Breakfast"

This would seem to agree with Northrop Frye's contention that literature does not mirror life but "swallows" it. Like Margaret Avison and A.M. Klein and Irving Layton before her, MacEwen puts considerable stress on the creative sense perception of the universe, on the universe as a place of wonder and continuing inner discover. Her poet is Klein's "nth Adam" who re-creates the world in his own poetic cosmos. Her Adam is the dancer in reverse dancing down his own throat, discovering "delicate fables of the flesh" ("The Two Themes of the Dance").

A Breakfast for Barbarians, MacEwen's first really successful book, continues the theme of "intake," of the poet as "I Interior," that was begun in the more precocious *Rising Fire*. The swimmer, the astronaut, the dancer, the magician—these recur as images of the poet whose activity is mythmaking, the construction from experience of meaningful patterns. MacEwen continues to promote the "appetite" that will restore man's relationship to the forbidding and apparently inhuman external world of his own inventions. This involves an expansion of consciousness that re-creates the world and helps to create the self—a process that assumes more openly nationalistic overtones in the work of Margaret Atwood. In "The Self Assumes" the poet describes the willful hunger of the soul, though it is uncertain whether she understands fully the dangers of such "will," proclaiming "the accurate self which burns, and burning, assumes green." The individual discovery of the universe is also the creation of the universe (Jung's "second cosmogony"). MacEwen's poet is by turns winemaker or magician or an escape artist who finds his way to a new heaven and earth. In "Black Alchemy" she imagines a second Adam who "cancels the cosmos," for "in his dance/Worlds expire like tides, in his flaming/dance the nameless cosmos/must await his naming."

In *The Shadow-Maker* MacEwen's exuberance disappears; there is a descent into darkness, a grappling with the problem of evil, and even something of an attempt to come to terms with Canada, that is, this world, the one we have to live in. In *The Armies of the Moon* a balance seems to have been restored: dark and light, divine and human, exotic and immediate find integration once again in "The Nine Arcana of the Kings," a powerful sequence which plays a variation on part of the story of MacEwen's novel *King of Egypt, King of Dreams*.

Certain questions arise in contemplating the work of MacEwen the poet. She began like Leonard Cohen as an adolescent prodigy and has continued as a more or less "natural" writer—she was decidedly not a slow learner. Her poems have a marvellous ease and energy, but sometimes they seem to lack overall shape. Also, there seems to be something of an imbalance in the direction of the inner life here. How much, the reader may ask, has the imaginative journeying to exotic worlds been a kind of romantic evasion of the realities and problems of her own time and place? On a vaster plane, MacEwen may not always be sufficiently aware of the trickiness, the humour, the *irony* of the God she addresses.

At times clearly, and in her best work, she is aware of the tensions and dangers of her situation and her chosen stance. Early on she writes:

> O baby, what Hell to be Greek in this country—
> without wings, but burning anyway

"Poem Improvised around a First Line"

And in a few poems in *The Shadow-Maker* she attempts to remedy this situation by addressing Canada itself as an exotic mystery. This is Magic Canada, a world of mystery and possibility. It is an open world with no final certainties or symmetries. In the prose piece "Kingsmere" MacEwen remarks upon the tension between past and future created by Mackenzie King's imposition of fake European ruins on the Canadian landscape. Through his stone arch is the forest, the native's past, and the mysterious future: the Indians perhaps were Canada's real Greeks. But Canadians will re-create eternal and archetypal patterns in their own way, or so MacEwen's book of stories *Noman* would seem to suggest. It is not necessary for her to paint herself into an exotic Egyptian or Greek corner.

The early, somewhat immature novel *Julian the Magician* concerns a man who is taken over by the divinity he cannot control. The more mature *King of Egypt, King of Dreams* tells MacEwen's version of the story of the pharoah Akhenaton, who may have been the first monotheist; indeed, the novel may be taken as a warning of the dangers of monotheism, of God conceived of only as light. It is, in this respect, a companion-piece to *The Shadow-Maker*. The one universal god is too masculine and rational to fulfil the emotional needs of the people, and is a source of terrible frustration to Akhenaton's beautiful queen and sister Nefertiti, who is driven by inner compulsions to infidelity and suicide. Akhenaton himself refuses to acknowledge the dark side of his nature and the material and temporal responsibility of his empire; consequently, these overwhelm him, and he goes to his moonlit death in the desert dressed as a woman. Akhenaton's probable father and eventual successor, the unheroic but capable Ay, is more "Canadian," however, in his scepticism, his ability to see several sides of every issue, his ability to see the complexity of the world and of the Word. Monotheism is perceived as a kind of psychic totalitarianism that denies the reality of one's dark, variable, and potentially violent self. For in MacEwen's whole work, as in much Canadian writing, there is an affirmation of the splendour of life that fully comprehends the horror.

King of Egypt is not without faults. It moves very slowly for the first third or so of the way and has over-ponderous moments thereafter. But the experience of Akhenaton, Ay's late reflections upon it, and the love story of

Smenkhare and Meritaton, subject also of MacEwen's finest long poem "The Nine Arcana of the Kings," are all-absorbing for the reader interested in the psychology of religious and erotic experience. Ay concludes: "Akhenaton was a lie. . . . It is a lie to assume there is only light, only goodness," for "the holy and the obscene exist side by side" and "beneath the bright heart of a man is the dark underworld of his soul" (Macmillan, p. 235). Good and evil, light and darkness are seen as interdependent and inescapably linked: this is the Jungian theme which *King of Egypt* shares with *The Double Hook* and *The Deserter*. Akhenaton "never permitted himself to reveal that underworld full of the creeping crawling things like violence or bitterness which all men must contain. He distorted those evils and let them build up within him until they emerged in grotesque, insane disguises" (p. 235). Thus he exemplifies an extreme human possibility, like one of Cohen's saints or Ondaatje's tragic heroes. *King of Egypt* unfolds a dramatic tale of considerable psychological significance with great skill and is a more remarkable fictional achievement than most readers and critics seem yet to have realized.

MacEwen could be accused of evading, as Ondaatje does, the more immediate realities of life in Canada, were it not for certain poems (particularly "Dark Pines under Water" and "The Discovery") and the stories of *Noman*, which is dedicated to "all the strangers in Kanada." Here the re-living of archetypal experiences in Canadian terms seems to be the unifying theme and underlying psychic necessity for writer and reader alike, something that MacEwen may well develop further in future fictions.

Still, she has for the most part, and again like Ondaatje, created her own "other world." Both seem more responsive to an inner vision than to any very defined contemporary social context. They are poets of dream. By way of contrast, Margaret Atwood and David Helwig, the remaining poet-novelists of note in this generation, address themselves to current social issues. In Atwood's work inner and outer worlds are balanced, and in Helwig's work the inner life tends to be subordinate to a hard look at the outer world, at least until recently. For this reason they are perhaps the most traditionally "novelistic" of the poet-novelists, but at the same time their work has characteristics, faults, and virtues akin to those found in the fictions of the others.

Atwood under and above Water

Somewhat more fortunate with the mass public than Gwendolyn MacEwen, partly because of her more or less direct espousal of contemporary feminist and nationalist aims, is that other dark lady of Canadian letters, Margaret Atwood. In her love of wilderness combined with cultural sophistication she embodies that basic Canadian paradox perceived in Isabella Crawford, D.C. Scott, E.J. Pratt, Earle Birney, Al Purdy, and a number of other writers. She has learned from Canadian predecessors of all kinds as well as from the international Gothic and popular tradition, working consciously within the Canadian tradition—one that may be defined or interpreted in different ways but which is definitely there to be examined.

Atwood is a swimmer. The familiar Canadian "underwater" motif, the notion of the self and Canada itself trapped underwater like Atlantis, occurs in the first poems of her first full collection and is repeated throughout her work, reaching a kind of climax in the novel *Surfacing*. The notions of inner order and outer space, garrison and wilderness, the issue of perspective and of the ways of seeing also recur, as they do in the work of Avison, Page and numerous other writers. Like Al Purdy and others, she has a concern for ancestors and for evolution, even for the geological past. There is the familiar Canadian identification with animals and a sense of fierce native gods. There is both social satire and an interest in the metaphysics of landscape, as in the work of P.K. Page. It is interesting that both have written effectively of landladies. There is that dislike of camera-images, of too precise or too fixed definitions that is found as well in the work of Avison, Purdy, Ondaatje, and many other contemporary writers. But there is no need to go on. Atwood utilizes Canadian traditions in an apparently more conscious way than most writers of her generation. She taps Canadian culture's most important concerns. And she brings to traditional materials her own sensibility, her own way of saying things: the famous cool, apparently detached tone, the canny disposition of loaded words in short, punchy lines without much heightening of rhythm. It is a style highly distinctive both in its limitations and its strengths. Atwood attempts, for better and/or worse, and certainly to her immediate advantage with readers, to clarify what is complex and difficult, to get right to what she regards as the essential point.

Metaphysics and metaphor: the search for ways in which to find one's whole self, to find identity with one's body, one's instincts, one's country—in this emotional pioneering Atwood moves to the centre of national concerns. The quest is both personal:

> Meanwhile on several
> areas of my skin, strange bruises glow
> and fade, and I can't remember
> what accidents I had, whether I was
> badly hurt, how long ago
>
> "What Happened"

and national, as in *The Journals of Susanna Moodie*. It's of interest here that the poem "What Happened," with its suggestion of amnesia, looks forward to the problems of the woman in *Surfacing*.

Atwood's protagonist is imprisoned in the haunted house of Canadian exile but also, and perhaps more fundamentally, she is imprisoned in time and by the sense of her own mortality, which adds a universal dimension to her predicament. In an early poem with a fairy-tale motif a dwarf keeps a maiden prisoner in a glass coffin. The conclusion of "The Circle Game" also suggests a stifling enclosure:

> I want to break
> these bones, your prisoning rhythms
>   (winter,
>   summer)
> all the glass cases,
>
> erase all maps,
> crack the protecting
> eggshell of your turning
> singing children:
>
> I want the circle
> broken.

The protagonist searches for a larger self, a truer identity; she wants to substitute a giant for the dwarf, to fill the space that dwarfs us. In "A Voice" Atwood imagines the giant who occupies and fills the space that we are merely "in." In "A Place: Fragments" she describes the Canadian as one who lives in a house of ice in order to survive; his land is not firm but fluid, moving; and he finds himself in a state of perpetual flux and confusion too, as if he were in outer space. But perhaps there is something further that is

> not lost or hidden
> but just not found yet
>
> that informs, holds together
> this confusion, this largeness
> and dissolving:
>
> not above or behind
> or within it, but one
> with it: an
>
> identity:
> something too huge and simple
> for us to see.

In the ecological fable "The Green Giant Murder," however, Atwood raises the possibility that the country may already have been murdered, and in "Backdrop Addresses Cowboy," she points out the way in which the American "hero" has desecrated the space he ought to have held sacred.

In "Progressive Insanities of a Pioneer," one of her best early poems, Atwood attacks again the masculine desire to control and contain every-thing within straight lines (this looks forward to the role of the rationalist father in *Surfacing*):

> If he had known unstructured
> space is a deluge
> and stocked his log house-
> boat with all the animals
>
> even the wolves,
>
> he might have floated.

The pioneer must, Atwood says, assimilate the wilderness (and its gods) into his psychic garrison, his ark, and not attempt to deny it or fence it out. Then he may survive and be at home, having accepted the "flood," the dark, predatory and mysterious flux of life: it is a familiar Canadian moral.

The Journals of Susanna Moodie enlarges upon the national theme; as a poem sequence it enlarges Atwood's scope and is highly successful, indeed an advance on her two earlier books, which were uneven though often striking. In the person and experience of Susanna Moodie the poet finds an appropriate objective correlative for her own thoughts and emotions. The book is both personal and objective, both nationalist and universal in its metaphysical enquiry. It has a power to move that the earlier fables of Frankenstein, green giants, and space-men did not have. Atwood's Moodie enters "a large darkness," the new land that forces her to confront her own darkness or deeper self until her mind and her established social ego are entered upon by darkness and by animals. She becomes an ark. Then in leaving the bush after seven years she loses much of the insight she has not quite grasped. Later, however, she develops the Canadian double vision, perceiving both beauty and terror around and within her. After death she achieves union with the energies of place.

Procedures for Underground presents family poems, the deep well of childhood memories, the bush, Canada under water, the descent into the earth to recover the wisdom of the spirits of place, alienation in cities, travel, and marriage. It is a quieter book of individual poems with a quieter and, for some, a more enduring appeal than the one that follows. *Power Politics* is, as they say, something else again—an account of grim sexual warfare that restores all the Atwood bite and mordant humour. It makes surreal black comedy out of the historic difficulties of women and the destructive games, projections and illusions of modern lovers in a world built on war and the destruction of the environment. But in *You Are Happy*, which can be regarded as a kind of sequel, the Atwood protagonist moves forward toward a new country of relationship without false hopes, promises, defences, evasions, mythologies. The singularity, the uniqueness of things, of people, in the flux: this is something nameless, beyond language, as in *Surfacing*. One gives oneself to the flux.

> what
> they tried, we
> tried but could never do
> before . without blood, the killed
> heart . to take
> that risk, to offer life and remain
>
> alive, open yourself like this and become whole
>
> "Book of Ancestors"

It is an affirmative book, then. Even the first section, in which the protagonist expresses grief, regret, and remorse, as well as anger, over the failure of a past relationship, is warmer and more sympathetic than any of Atwood's earlier icy and often accurate analyses of the wicked ways of men, women and modern urban societies. Her new poems are earthier in the best and most positive sense. Technically, too, this book is an advance beyond *Power Politics*. Some of the shock-tactics and surreal effects of the earlier book are inadequate to the psychological processes they are attempting to represent. The later book's four sections move through yet another expression of the basic realities of hunger, death, and the predatory and through a further expression of sexual tension and the cruel fatalism of myth in terms of the story of Circe and Ulysses to the freer kind of relationship described above. The cruelty of myth has been left behind; the sacrifice and offering are voluntary, and in this there is freedom. In earlier Atwood collections even the body was regarded as a prison, but here it is singled out for praise. The book is a moving human statement, a journey. Indeed, Atwood's poetry to date represents a journey through darkness toward wholeness.

Her first two novels, *The Edible Woman* and *Surfacing*, are enlargements upon the themes of her poems. In each of them a young woman is driven to rebellion against what seems to be her fate in the modern technological "Americanized" world and to psychic breakdown and breakthrough. But they are quite different in tone and style.

The Edible Woman is delightfully, wickedly funny. It is feminist, certainly, but it provides a satirical account of the absurd ways of Canadian men *and* women. It is kindly in its irony: never so fierce in its assault as is *Power Politics*. There is anger but there is also good humour. The major characters are satirized—they represent various undesirable ways of existing in the modern consumer society—but they are also seen sympathetically as human beings, even the pompous Peter and the pathetic Lothario Leonard. They are not grotesque caricatures like David and Anna in *Surfacing*. The absurd superfemale Ainslie and the endlessly harassed mother Clara may have little in the way of guidance to offer Atwood's overly sensible heroine Marian, but each of them is shrewd enough to realize that she should not marry Peter.

Her body knows this too even as her mind accepts marriage. She finds herself unable to eat because she identifies with food. Indeed, she is Alice in Consumerland—there is even the mad dinner party with the graduate students to underline this suggestion. However, she finds a way out of her predicament with the help of the impossible Duncan, a fellow sufferer who seems to demand nothing of her but who may, it is hinted at the novel's ambivalent conclusion, become a future threat to her selfhood. But at least from now on Marian will struggle to achieve her true self; she will not easily be consumed by society or by any man.

This is a largely successful comic novel, even if the mechanics are some-times a little clumsy, the satirical accounts of consumerism a little drawn out. It is skilfully written, shifting easily from first to third person and back again to convey the stages of Marian's mental travels, her journey into self-alienation and out again. Of Atwood's three novels it is least a poet's novel.

In the larger context of Atwood's whole output to date, and of Canadian literature at large, the consumer society might be seen as an aspect of the predatory universe, a cosmic problem that Atwood does not attempt to solve. Running through her work, as we have seen, is the theme of discovery and the creation of self and of country, and this is, I believe, a major theme of Canadian literature at large, the more positive complement or aftermath of the notorious "victim" theme. There is a real wish to inhabit the body, the self, the country, to surface from the underwater world of fear, frustration and unfulfilment, to fill the space, waken the sleeping giant.

Surfacing introduces a young woman far more fearful, desperate, and alienated from her true self than Marian McAlpin. The atmosphere is correspondingly tense and eerie, for this is a psychological ghost story like *The Turn of the Screw*, in which the ghosts, the young woman's parents, are lost parts of herself that she must recover. She has been unable to feel for years, even though she had a good childhood, much of it spent on an island in northern Quebec. She believes (as the reader does for much of the book) that she has been married and divorced, abandoning a child. Her encounter with the gods of place and, apparently, with the corpse of her drowned father when she returns to the scene of her childhood reveals the truth—that she had in fact had a traumatic abortion—and this drives her to a healing madness, a descent to animal simplicity and a rejection of the destructive, mechanical "civilization" that has wounded her and of all its works, even words.

I can feel my lost child surfacing within me, forgiving me, rising from the lake where it has been prisoned for so long, its eyes and teeth phosphorescent; the two halves clasp, interlocking like fingers, it buds, it sends out fronds. This time I will do it by myself, squatting, on old newspapers in a corner alone; or on leaves, dry leaves, a heap of them, that's cleaner. The baby will slip out easily as an egg, a kitten, and I'll lick it off and bite the cord, the blood returning to the ground where it belongs; the moon will be full, pulling. In the morning I will be able to see it: it will be covered with shining fur, a god, I will never teach it any words (McClelland and Stewart, pp. 161-62).

The forest leaps upward, enormous, the way it was before they cut it, columns of sunlight frozen; the boulders float, melt, everything is made of water, even the rocks. In one of the languages there are no nouns, only verbs held for a longer moment.
The animals have no need for speech, why talk when you are a word.
I lean against a tree, I am a tree leaning.

I break out again into the bright sun and crumple, head against the ground.
I am not an animal or a tree, I am the thing in which the trees and animals move and grow, I am a place (p. 181).

Receiving the gods of place, and the spirits of her parents who have become the gods, *herself becoming place*, the Atwood protagonist receives strength and is able to return to her own time, to human civilization, to words. Her friends David and Anna may be machine-people, second-hand "Americans" (that is, wanton in psychological destructiveness, wholly ignorant of the spirits of the wild) and thus beyond redemption, but her lover Joe, inarticulate and baffled, is not yet corrupt and is perhaps the appropriate father for the child she believes they have conceived. At the novel's end the Atwood protagonist prepares to return to society as LePan's Rusty did. But she hopes that she carries the seed of the future, a vision of man and place in harmony, of the sleeping giant awakening, the larger consciousness surfacing.

Surfacing begins in a mundane enough way, but it then builds up an extraordinary tension and suspense as hints of a mystery far more profound than the physical disappearance of a father are offered. Atwood's repeated use of run-on sentences helps to establish the rhythm of her heroine's growing awareness and panic. The evocation of the bush, the lake, the islands is marvellously handled. A physical and spiritual journey is unfolded. It is like a Canadian version of James Dickey's *Deliverance*. The main character is a woman instead of a man; no-one is killed or raped; power-lust and violence are repudiated instead of reluctantly then enthusiastically adopted, as in the American "Western" tradition. If David and Anna are walking talking clichés rather than human beings, this is because that is how the narrator, however unfairly from any more complex perspective, comes to see them. The first-person point of view combined with the evocative description of setting makes it possible for Atwood to get away with a certain shallowness of characterization; only the narrator seems at all complex. But this is not something that interferes with the powerful flow of the novel as one reads it.

Still, it is evident here, as it is more seriously in *Lady Oracle*, the third novel, that characterization is not Atwood's strong point. And it is revealing that much of her fiction, including her shorter fiction, employs the first person. Everything must be filtered through the mind of the Atwood protagonist, who is usually supposed to be both shrewd and confused, a combination that is possible but which tends in certain cases to put some strain on the reader's credulity. In this respect *The Edible Woman* is a more balanced novel than *Surfacing*, and yet it is *Surfacing*, the poet's novel, that more powerfully engages the reader's emotions.

In *Surfacing* the repeated imagery of bottled, trapped and murdered animals builds powerfully to the key scene in which the father's corpse and the aborted foetus are encountered. The subsequent scenes of vision and madness are as vivid and metaphorical in language as much of *The Double Hook* or *The Deserter*; here is effective poetic technique in the novel. In *Lady Oracle*, however, a similar patterning of images, metaphors, and ideas fails to compensate for the fuzzy personality of the narrator, even if this last is part of the author's point. Nor is there the power of language found in the latter part of *Surfacing*. Indeed, the female-picaresque *Lady Oracle* is decidedly thinner than the other novels and lacking in over-all shape or focus, even if it is in places very interesting and enjoyable and even if it offers some rewarding insights into the need for and nature of art and the fantasy life. It is just that all of this seems too intellectually worked out, too far removed from any very deeply felt or imagined experience of the kind that "stood in," so to speak, for any very searching exploration of human character in *Surfacing*. Though a serious emotional resonance seems quite clearly intended, it is not achieved, mainly because recurrent poetic imagery is finally no substitute for depth of characterization. This is the major limitation of Atwood the novelist. Also, the reader may suspect that Atwood is indulging herself a little in this book, even to the extent of succumbing somewhat to the old-style "woman's fiction" she parodies: though surely the incisive cultural critic could never turn into Mazo de la Roche?

It is in *Surfacing*, where a considerable emotional power is allowed to develop (as in *The Journals of Susanna Moodie*, another excursion into "large darkness" and out again), that Atwood's vision and gifts may be seen to best advantage. Here she has given the theme of quest into darkness and the journey to wholeness, a theme that she shares in recent Canadian fiction with Klein, LePan, Watson, Cohen, and MacEwen, its most overtly Canadian expression, and this is no doubt one reason for her considerable success at a time when this great and universal theme has a special significance for a rapidly developing and "surfacing" Canadian consciousness.

Bourgeois and Arsonist

David Helwig

Moving from the work of Ondaatje to that of MacEwen to that of Atwood to that of David Helwig, the final poet-novelist under consideration, a reader discovers greater and greater consideration of and interest in the contemporary social world. Cohen has these interests, of course, but it is a significantly distorted version of that world that is presented in *Beautiful Losers*. Similarly, LePan attempts to deal with contemporary reality in *The Deserter* but in terms of an anonymous city and a virtually anonymous hero. Helwig is much more the literary realist than any of the above writers. At the same time, though, he is a poet whose work in poetry and prose reveals a vision that may usefully be compared to those already examined.

Helwig began as a poet of fact, as MacEwen and Ondaatje began, obviously, as poets of dream. Many of his early poems are domestic pieces, celebrations of the commonplace, the sharp joys and wonders of children and the outdoors. Most of these remain charming, easy to read and enter into. The writing is skilful and unobtrusive like the best shorter poems of William Carlos Williams or Raymond Souster. Helwig can use the plain style subtly and flexibly too. Other poems suggest the reason for such a patient and loving attention to the minute incidents of experience: only thus can the irrational and terrifying energies that inhabit and animate the world be given form and meaning. Helwig's poems appear to be spells against inner and outer chaos. There is an ambivalence in the description of the "arsonist" who runs across the bourgeois poet's front lawn as he watches from the window: the arsonist, whose "flaming" feet "dance," whose hair is "silent flame" and whose eyes "flash awake like a struck match" ("Reflections"). He is the source of joy and terror alike; he is an aspect of the self (like the ghosts in *Surfacing*), the primitive poet inside the tender husband and father of the domestic poems. The man inside the window, the dark other self outside: this seems to be Helwig's spontaneous rendering of the themes of garrison balanced by the wild and of self-integration that are so central to so many Canadian writers.

How is one to contain and live with the arsonist, to reconcile energy and form, freedom and order? As Helwig's work develops, this problem reveals a political and historical dimension but it remains a problem of human psychology, a universal problem addressed by Ondaatje, MacEwen, and Atwood in their own sometimes rather similar and sometimes quite different fashions. Of Edward Hicks, who painted "The Peaceable Kingdom" at least a hundred times, Helwig writes:

> You must have had violent hands
> to have needed so often,
> a hundred times at least,
> the magic, the talisman,
> the peaceable Kingdom
> made by your hands.
>
> "For Edward Hicks"

The artist is engaged then in the exorcism of his own and the world's violence. Perhaps Canada is frequently labelled "the peaceable kingdom" partly because its people are so aware, in some deep, instinctive way, of the potential and actual violence of place and people. In "The Dream Book," one of the most interesting of Helwig's early, somewhat untheatrical short plays, the young hero fails to risk himself and to face "the vistas of horror and beauty" that would be opened up by the vision of the "murdered god." He feels he is a poet, but he is unable to write a single word because he is obsessed by the fate of Orpheus, the price of such a dangerous vocation. He must therefore live in silence and self-denial.

By way of contrast, Helwig himself moves closer and closer to terror, to the depiction of man's inhumanity to man, the problem of human aggression, the long injustice of history, the loneliness of the individual, the difficulties of human relationship. He moves out from the domestic island to the larger concerns of our human and cultural situation, and also, more recently, inward to the kind of violent psychic landscape that Ondaatje has long made his particular territory, that is, to the heart of the human problem. In his early explorations, Helwig himself remained too sane, more certain in his conclusions than the mysterious and multidimensional world would seem to warrant. Certainly, there is no Orphic or Dionysian frenzy or "letting go." But his latest work reveals more awareness of the limits of rational definition. It seeks a language for the larger silence (or "absence" or "cadence," to use Dennis Lee's terms for the ultimately mysterious larger rhythm of things).

In the title poem of the collection *The Best Name of Silence*, the Bluebeard story is retold as an exploration of sexual psychology. This is certainly not a new way of handling it, but the very fine speeches given to Bluebeard and his latest wife powerfully convey the deadly fascination of the total knowledge of the beloved which leads ultimately to silence and death. It is a story that happens over and over or else the beginning of all stories, an ancient mystery. Still, the experience is conveyed in a distanced way, as conscious and formal artifice. A more ambitious, more vivid, more immediately dramatic and even darker exploration of human courage and pain is the four-part *Atlantic Crossings*, which concerns the voyages to the new world of St. Brendan, a slave-trader, Christopher Columbus, and the Norse.

The speaker of "Voyage with Brendan" is a follower, a peasant who can perceive things spiritual only dimly as they are reflected in Brendan. He is bought and taken from his bestial hovel by monks who instruct him, though he is uncomprehending, in the existence and mysteries of the soul. He then leaves with Brendan for the voyage. They visit an island that turns out to be a whale and then visit other visionary islands. Leviathan, the great beast of Revelations, is defeated by God's dragon in a sea-battle and devoured; Judas is encountered "on holiday from hell." Having received Brendan's visionary experience, the narrator is cast up alone on a North American coast where an Indian smelling of animals approaches him. The language and syntax in this first section are stripped down, bare, as in some of Michael Ondaatje's poems; the effect is similarly vivid, sensuous, kinetic. There is no editorializing. What Brendan's vision will mean to life in the new land is not clear at this point.

"'The Middle Passage" is the stunning monologue of the captain of a slave-ship. It is more sensuous, immediate, and powerful than anything else Helwig has written. The captain represents an extreme "masculine" drive for dominance and money; the black woman whose arms and legs are tied to the four corners of his cabin is seen as the earth and as his creation. Driven mad by the foul calm of this shark-infested sea-world and the ugly disease-ridden enterprise over which "the breath of God" has been "breathed back and held" (that is, withheld), he kills the woman with a knife in a more or less spontaneous or automatic fashion, then lies on her, carrying the power mania of Western man to its logical sexual conclusion. A mass rape of the slave women by the sailors has occurred already.

"Columbus in Jamaica," the third part of this poetic symphony, is a different kind of monologue, Columbus's complaint in adversity. Religion, or religiosity, and commercial greed are both elements of the great admiral's character as his surviving writings indicate. He combines the psychic imperialism of Christianity with the commercial imperialism that is seen at its worst in the slave-trade. Helwig's Columbus is a megalomaniac suffering from the delusions of fever, bitter over the ingratitude of his royal masters in Spain. He embodies, as he did in life, the transition from medieval to modern times.

The speaker of "The Vinland Saga" is a woman, which gives a different perspective on the experience of encounter with a new world. With her second husband, Karlsefni, Gudrid journeys west to the New World, where she gives birth to a son. Violent conflict with the Indians follows upon trade with them, so they return home across the ocean. Freydis, a fiercer woman, goes again to the new land, however, where she kills out of greed. Gudrid comments, "She left our mark on the land." Gudrid espouses a saner life of continual renewal, of endless communion with her own land:

> Each night
> I bury fire under its grey ash,
> and in the morning breathe it into life.
> I tell my sons the stories of the gods,
> of Christ coming up out of the earth,
> Baldur young and beautiful from the sea.

These simple values are posed against the history of exploitation and conquest and lust for the absolute that run through the four poems, but no historical or political solution is offered, since it seems a little late for most Canadians to go back to Europe, only a close examination of the beginnings of our North American experience.

Atlantic Crossings is highly successful. Helwig's earlier poetry was powerful, too, especially in its very striking descriptive and visual effects. But certain mannerisms did not always wear well. Certain repetitions of rhythms and phrases can seem overdone; what George Johnston in a recent review called Helwig's steady "no nonsense" tone is often too definite, too self-insistent in its assertion of what is. Again, the deliberate artifice of the "art" poems, the mythological trappings and masks, were not always very illuminating. But these are minor and occasional complaints; for the most part a powerful vision and sensibility are unfolded. In *Atlantic Crossings* the vision deepens as the poet's own personality recedes a little; there is a sense of the violence and mystery at the heart of things, as in MacEwen and Ondaatje; there is a near-perfect mastery of tone, setting and incident, and an intricate musical structure.

Helwig's fiction has the same virtues as his best poetry, particularly the paramount virtue of clarity, of clear seeing. Most of his stories are very brief, significant moments in the lives of apparently very ordinary people. But while they are good, they are not very exciting (Clarke Blaise found them maddeningly "Chekhovian").¹ One, however, the superb novella or long story, "The Streets of Summer," is much more ambitious. It concerns a love-triangle: the sober graduate student, John, who wants to learn how to be truly young one fateful summer; the emotionally wounded Sonya, who needs to feel that every man loves her but cannot love in return; the despairing suicidal actor Matt, who is the eventual victim of his own and John's hopeless love for the sympathetic but ultimately faithless Sonya. Each character is unfolded gradually until it is clear that all three are emotionally insufficient. Sonya has been incapacitated by her childhood in the concentration camp to which her Nazi father has consigned her mother. Matt believes that he is a failure as an actor and drinks too much; he despairs of his union with Sonya even though he sleeps with her. John, apparently the dullest but really the most dangerous of the three, is the "boy scout" doggedly determined to "reach" and win Sonya at the same time as he resents the destruction of his petty "order" that is brought about by his involvement with the disturbed lovers. John and Matt (with his iconoclasm, his bitter wit, and his death-wish) are the boy scout and the arsonist respectively, two of the selves revealed in Helwig's poetry. Sonya, for her part, seems to represent the passivity and extreme emotional insecurity of all those numbed by the horror of contemporary history. But all three are sharply individualized and made humanly sympathetic as well.

In *The Day before Tomorrow*, Helwig's first novel, however, the notion of "revolution" tossed about by some of its characters seems ill-defined and probably sentimental, and thus not worth Helwig's sustained attention. More than this, none of the major characters are very sympathetic. One is a tense, somewhat morose, and indeed slightly obnoxious university student with something of a chip on his shoulder; but he is idealistic, if personally selfish. Next, there is a frigid woman with an obsession about what she regards as "religion." In addition, there are some paper revolutionaries, who plot theatrical demonstrations, and finally, a sexually disturbed diplo-mat who becomes a spy. He is by far the most likeable and interesting character. Their story is very well written, as one would expect, but not always very interesting. The book comes most alive when it is given over to the journals of John Martens, the diplomat, who becomes a spy in order to contribute his own small bit, sacrificing his own emotional and mental stability to the process of "history" (as conceived by Marx). The journal is lively and aphoristic—the self-portrait of a disturbed and brilliant man driven to desperation and paranoid fantasy by his son's death, his wife's consequent total sexual withdrawal, and his notion of entering history. He writes:

A man wishes to care for his family and knows instinctively that this is a right action, a moral action. But he cares for them, in most cases, by being party to the oppression of other men, other children. What happened to me was that suddenly, knowing myself as a childless man married to a woman who cared for nothing but what was dead, I could see clearly that there was no time to wait, that the future had lost its meaning for me unless I reached out and deliberately grasped a future that mattered. I became a political man (Oberon, p. 57).

Here the bourgeois becomes the arsonist. Inevitably, John comes to grief in this fashion, and he is deluded in any case, since it is apparently the military designs of the Russian Empire that his spying serves. However, his younger brother Jake, smart-alecky and unattractive though he is, persists, after observing the operations of squatters in London, England, in the idealistic and admirable belief that some transformation of human values and some practical action in that direction remain possible. He resolves vaguely to get some sort of practical operation going back home in Kingston, Ontario.

Helwig once said that while his first novel had to do with his quarrel with Marx, the second was to express his quarrel with Freud. But it seems less a quarrel than a capitulation to some of Freud's most pessimistic observations about human sexuality. And the result is, indeed, a most unhappy love story, the tale of a separated, fortyish man and a neurotic young girl. It is also very good. Called *The Glass Knight*, it makes more use of Kingston's special atmosphere and physical character than *The Day before Tomorrow*. The young girl, Elizabeth, is, like the older Margaret in the first novel, frigid. The man's attempt to win her results only in a kind of rape. He can at times compel her sexual response, but this only brings on serious emotional side-effects and then her flight to a lesbian friend in England. It is a depressing tale, but the atmosphere of Kingston, the lake, the old houses, the sense of ghosts in the streets, is superbly captured. Helwig now thinks that this is the first of several related novels: such a series could be as masterful as *Atlantic Crossings*. He has, like Atwood, produced a remarkable and varied body of work in a relatively short time.

The Glass Knight, lyrical and atmospheric, is probably too constricted in scope to be comparable to the significant fictions of the other poet-novelists. Still, it explores sexuality and sexual obsessions in as intense a way as does the work of LePan, Cohen, Ondaatje, and MacEwen. *The Day before Tomorrow* is more ambitious in scope, enlarging upon the concern for violence and man's tragic complexity that characterizes Helwig's most impressive poems in a fashion that is comparable to that of *The Second Scroll, The Double Hook, The Deserter, Beautiful Losers, King of Egypt, King of Dreams,* and *Surfacing*, all of which have social as well as psychological implications. But it is much less resonant, less a parable than any of these, achieving a comparable degree of poetic intensity and compression only in the first-person diaries of Helwig's spy. Probably there should have been more of this eloquent paranoia; that is, this novel might benefit from being more a poet's novel than it is, for such manic wit or vision is precisely what underlines serious ideas in most of these works, whether it is Klein's Uncle Melech in his letter on the Sistine Chapel, LePan's omniscient account of Rusty's super-charged consciousness, the ravings of Cohen's F. or his narrator, the visions of MacEwen's Akhenaton, or the final ecstasies of Atwood's narrator that the reader overhears. *The Day before Tomorrow* might have been stronger if the author had given the deeply disturbed John a freer rein.

But then, not one of these novels is of the same order of achievement as, say, *As for Me and My House, The Mountain and the Valley, The Sacrifice* or *The Stone Angel.* Nor could it be said that these writers, even Cohen and Atwood, their celebrity notwithstanding, are yet as significant as novelists as F.P. Grove, Morley Callaghan, Hugh MacLennan, Robertson Davies, Margaret Laurence, or Mordecai Richler. As poets alone, moreover, they cannot match the achievement of our finest living poets: Earle Birney, Irving Layton, Margaret Avison, and Al Purdy. But there is a peculiar power and interest, nevertheless, in their work because a "poetry"—a vivid, heightened, sensuous language or a metaphorical and symbolic compression of narrative and structure—infuses the flawed novels, which themselves cast new light on the authors' poems. A largeness of vision absent in most of our less technically adventurous poets is thus revealed.

The poet-novelists have helped to enlarge in Canada the possibilities of fiction. The mixing of prose and poetry in single works, the sense of fragmentation conveyed in other ways are in themselves expressive of a recognition of discrete, individual things ("There is only one of everything," writes Atwood) and also of a longing for identity, integrity, unity with some whole. In Klein, LePan, and Atwood, these are primarily expressed in imagery, metaphor and a sensuous heightened flow of language; in Cohen, Ondaatje, MacEwen, and Helwig, primarily as narrative technique. Put me together, such novels say, even as they say (as Cohen's F. does) "connect nothing." The most experimental (or in some cases, startling) new Canadian fiction of such as Graeme Gibson (*Five Legs,* 1969), Scott Symons (*Place d'Armes,* 1967), Dave Godfrey (*The New Ancestors,* 1970), Matt Cohen (*The Disinherited,* 1974), Rudy Wiebe (*The Temptations of Big Bear,* 1973), and Marian Engel (*Bear,* 1976) reveals a similar concern for re-integration and shows affinity with or, in some cases, quite definite influence of the poet's novels, most especially *Beautiful*

Losers. The New Ancestors won the Governor General's award for fiction in the same year that *Billy the Kid* won the award for poetry. Like Ondaatje, Godfrey creates a unique imaginative world, one that is pungent, hallucinatory and kaleidoscopic in atmosphere, by means of fragmented narrative, but much more substantially and at greater length, and he presents characters charged by anger, grief, frustration and madness. Both writers have surely been influenced, or at the very least reinforced in their projects by *Beautiful Losers* as well as by writers from abroad, for Cohen pioneered in Canadian fiction, as his predecessor, Layton, had done in poetry, a new freedom in the treatment of matters sexual and also a new stylistic and structural freedom. He helped to make possible the sexual frankness and the dual or multiple perspective in narrative technique that is common to *Place d'Armes, Five Legs, The New Ancestors, The Disinherited,* and *The Temptations of Big Bear*, in each of which various characters are allowed to develop their view of things at length. Again, there are passages of highly sensuous and poetic language, frequently involving a dense interior monologue, and of surreal intensity in each of these novels. In a different way *Bear,* a more conventionally structured parable of the encounter with the wild written in a quite straightforward and lucid style, is obviously indebted to *Surfacing*. Ironically, or perhaps typically, *Bear* is more perfectly executed but less moving than *Surfacing*.

Perhaps these new developments in the Canadian novel would have occurred even without the participation of the poets, simply because it was time for them after the more traditional achievements of Callaghan, MacLennan, Laurence, Richler, and others and because young Canadian writers were looking with great interest at the fictional experiments of such as Burroughs, Pynchon, and others abroad. But it is significant that poets Cohen and Ondaatje should be so central in this movement in Canada and that the older poets Klein and LePan, with their flawed but gorgeous and boldly baroque fictions, should have helped to point the way. It is significant that this new fiction blossomed in Canada in the dynamic 1960's and 1970's and with certain poets in the vanguard.

This quest into darkness and the return to community thus facilitated by poetic means has national implications. Twenty years after the war that was supposed to have greatly advanced Canada's progress to nationhood there was indeed an intensified consciousness of the glory and the danger of life in this northern space. "Put me together," says *Beautiful Losers*, a work that embodies in its characters and structure Canada's fractured psyche, emphasizing the force of the past and the force of modern America within it. The themes of integration and potential community that were always paramount in our poetry receive new technical emphasis in the new poet's-fiction of the dark and the light of existence. An increasingly self-conscious Canada in the dangerous postwar world dominated by the American empire is once again engaged in the old and universal quest for self-knowledge. In the fiction of the poet this quest is usually rendered less in social terms than in terms of fable or parable that can convey the interior life, the terrors and aspirations of Canadians. The exterior social world had been and was being dealt with more substantially by Callaghan, MacLennan, Davies, Laurence and Richler. Looked at in another way, though, the movement of the poets—even, perhaps, for Ondaatje—to fiction can be seen as a movement outward from that lyrical ghettoization that seemed to be the fate promised in Klein's "Portrait of the Poet as Landscape" toward a fuller sense of community and a fuller communication and revelation of the interior life of everyone. That is its largest significance.

Notes

1. Clarke Blaise, review of *The Streets of Summer, Quarry* 19, no. 3 (1970).

CONCLUSION

There are so many at least competent poets writing and publishing in Canada today that predictions are rash. Certain continuities and developments, however, can be observed.

There are now a great number of good woman poets working in Canada. Isabella Crawford is their Canadian ancestor. Later Dorothy Livesay held the fort virtually alone. Then Margaret Avison, P.K. Page, Miriam Waddington, and Jay Macpherson achieved considerable and deserved prominence. The sixties brought us two queens of the new poetry of that time—MacEwen and Atwood. All of these poets have been concerned to some degree with a woman's experience and perspective, and therefore can be considered as "woman poets" for the moment, even though they are excellent poets by any standard. They help to correct an imbalance and to give us a broader view of life in Canada. These days one expects poets as individual and accomplished as the late Pat Lowther or Susan Musgrave to turn up regularly as a matter of course. It is another aspect, aided and abetted by the women's movement, of the explosion of new talent that still goes on.

Some of our younger poets are more ambitious than most of their immediate predecessors; they are thinking in terms of larger structures, even if they are not also novelists. A random and certainly incomplete list of larger poems or poem-sequences, some of them book-length, many of them re-creations of Canadian history in the tradition of Pratt but in a freer and less constricted idiom, demonstrates this: Gary Geddes's *War and Other Measures,* Victor Coleman's *America,* Don Gutteridge's *Riel,* b.p. nichol's *The Martyrology,* Dennis Lee's *Civil Elegies* and his *Death of Harold Ladoo,* numerous long poems or sequences by Frank Davey, George Bowering, Lionel Kearns, and Daphne Marlatt, John Robert Colombo's compilations of "found" material, Stuart MacKinnon's *The Intervals,* Florence McNeil's *Emily,* Gail Fox's "Flight of the Pterodactyl", Wayne Clifford's "Passages," George McWhirter's *Catalan Poems*, Terry Crawford's *The Werewolf Miracles,* Douglas Barbour's *A Poem As Long As the Highway,* Peter Stevens's *And the Dying Sky Like Blood,* which concerns Norman Bethune, J. Michael Yates's *The Great Bear Lake Meditations*, Sid Stephen's *Beothuk Poems*, and the late John Thompson's

Stilt Jack. Atwood's Moodie sequence, Ondaatje's narratives, and Helwig's *Atlantic Crossings* have been discussed already.

Dennis Lee's *Civil Elegies,* formally and stylistically indebted to Eliot's *Four Quartets* and Rilke's *Duino Elegies* and intellectually beholden to the theories of George Grant, is one of the most timely and interesting of such longer poems. Just as striking in another way, though, and perhaps more durable, and certainly as indicative of the ongoing development of Canadian poetry, are some of Lee's shorter poems, whose flexible and canny lining renders the sense of objects in movement in space, some universal cadence (as Lee calls it), drift or flux uncannily well. He does not sound like Purdy or Avison, but he has evolved a similarly persuasive and flowing idiom:

> The low-light recedes, the records recede, skin
>   empties. Under my eyes
> your eyes recede, I brush your cheek you feel what
>   touch what clumsy much-loved man
> receding? Your body is full of listening,
>   exquisite among its own
> shockwaves. So. What
>   space are you going into?
>
> "When It Is Over"

Purdy is recalled once again as the reader experiences the free-flowing, run-on poems of David McFadden, the proletarian, frequently comic narratives of Tom Wayman, or the ongoing life of the prairies and mountains as rendered by Dale Zieroth, Sid Marty, Andrew Suknaski, and Patrick Lane. He is brought to mind too by the precise love poems of Ian Young, the cheerfully mordant wit of George Jonas, and the zany ramblings among the flowerbeds of Joe Rosenblatt. There is a new freedom and ease with the long or short free-verse line, a flow, a sense of the world in endless Heraclitean flux that seems a natural and inevitable development from the idiom and insights of Purdy and Avison.

This poetic process seems to me to be one that comes naturally from the experience of the open Canadian land and the likeliest path to further exploration of our physical and psychic space in future. Such a line of development is more central and important to Canadians than the so-called Black Mountain poetics so enthusiastically adopted and touted by a number of poets of the 1960's and 1970's, particularly in Vancouver. Not that these latter are without worth. The American B.M. theories may well be of use just as the imagism of an earlier time has been of use, and they may even be consistent in their way with what has happened earlier in Canada, but they are not crucial to our native development. Since large claims have been made for them, however, particularly by Warren Tallman, the American high priest of the B.M. tribe of poets in Vancouver, perhaps the matter should be examined at least briefly in a book dealing with the phases of Canadian poetry.

The Black Mountain. What is it? Firstly, it is the theory and practice of certain American poets: Charles Olson, Robert Duncan and Robert Creeley, in particular. Behind Olson stands Ezra Pound, behind Creeley, William Carlos Williams. These earlier poets, of course, had their effect on Dudek and Souster in the previous generation. Here, though, the Black Mountain is the theory and practice of certain American poets as understood and emulated by certain Canadian poets, most of them centred in Vancouver. A recent handy and near-definitive guide to this movement is Warren Tallman's article "Wonder Merchants: Modernist Poetry in Vancouver during the 1960's."[1]

As Tallman's account reveals, it was a group of aspiring young academics and poets—George Bowering, Frank Davey and Lionel Kearns among them—who formed a study group in 1961 to discuss the American poetry prescribed for them by the visiting Robert Duncan. Later they founded a newsletter called anagramatically *Tish*. Tallman suggests that the young poets of the West eagerly seized on this particular strain of American poetry, which had yet to become established and accepted to any degree in the United States, because of the experience of the unsettled wilderness of mountains and interior and ocean, the "manifest reaches of humanly untouched space." He seems here to be unaware that all important Canadian poets past and present from all parts of the country have been obsessed with wilderness and space. This is one reason why imagism in some form has been important everywhere in Canada.

Tallman's account of what is distinctive about Black Mountain poetry may or may not have the assent of all its practitioners, but it is an interesting one. He says that it is "proprioceptive" instead of merely "perceptive": "The perceptive writer sees himself in the midst of the surrounding world as object. The proprioceptive writer sees the surrounding world in the midst of himself as subject—'sensibility within the organism.'" Tallman feels, perhaps rightly, that such a process transcends ordinary egotism and despair. The proprioceptive writer, he says, "incorporates" his place into himself: Olson and his internalized Gloucester, Massachusetts, provide one good example.

This internalization of the world is the tendency of a great deal of poetry since the Romantic revolution in sensibility almost two centuries ago; and no doubt it was always present in some sense even before that, whatever the poet—Dante, say—consciously thought he was doing. Since 1800 or so there is increasing interest in the process of perception, the process of taking-the-world-in in order to feel at one with it. Surely Wordsworth was moving in this direction with his exploration of world and self in *The Prelude*, and surely his "egotistical sublime" (as Keats had it) leads directly to Whitman, who sings of America-as-Walt and is easily as "proprioceptive" as Charles Olson. Tallman speaks of "the wonder that came bubbling up from within," echoing, perhaps unconsciously, D.H. Lawrence's "Song of a Man Who Has Come Through." This is not an experience unknown to poets who are not fully persuaded by Black Mountain theology and hagiography, nor are they without knowledge of the world and, especially, of other people as experienced in themselves or of the necessity of expressing this as poetic form. Klein's "Portrait of the Poet as Landscape" has the insight, if not the form, and Avison and Purdy are able, emotionally and technically, to be "proprioceptive" or not as they please.

There can be no objection, then, to "proprioception" as an idea or a method. What is irritating is the implicit assumption that—as practised by the Americans and their Vancouver followers—it is The Method, that no other possibility remains, that only a certain group of poets has The Truth, that no others can have thought and lived the contemporary situation through to any other method or conclusion. Such attitudes represent not openness, as the B.M. theologians maintain, but dogma and a new defensiveness. Tallman writes accurately that Canadian "eclecticism points to that open catholicity of mind which is the most conspicuous and appealing trait of intelligence in Canada. In a country that has grown up surrounded by an English and a French and an American fact, many of the best minds become capable of handling multiplicity sympathetically without the need to choose up sides and start yelling. Multiple-city"; but then he goes on (in upper case, as if to emphasize that this is one of the unquestionable commandments from the Mountain), "THERE IS A TIDE OR UNDERTOW THROUGHOUT THE MODERN WORLD WHICH MAKES THE ECLECTIC POSITION MORE AND MORE DIFFICULT TO MAINTAIN." He neglects to say what this "tide" is; fortunately for him, given his vagueness about a key issue, he takes the trouble to dissociate himself from American nationalism and imperialism and to insist that the mysterious "tide" is "international."

There may or may not be any such tide sweeping the B.M. to inevitable world ascendancy and empire. I suspect that history will have as many surprises in the future as in the past. As for Canadian eclecticism, it leads to or yields up something beyond itself in the work of Purdy and Avison: an idiom (different in each case) that is open and flexible enough to contend with the variegated and multidimensional Canadian reality, and beyond that, with the multidimensional and variegated world. The younger poets of the Black Mountain persuasion do not seem to me to have this kind of flexibility and command, but then it is not developed overnight. I think that they may well learn more in the end, if they can outgrow the need for dogma, from these poets than from the messianic American insistence on One Way for all mankind. How is it that American individualism, as expressed, say, in Tallman's notion of proprioception, so easily becomes messianic proselytizing? Surely this psychological complex is something "American." Tallman's essay is brilliant and engaging, like all his criticism, but ultimately too partisan and too involved in the promotion of personal friends and protegés to be taken as the last word; that is, it is as subjective as this present account of fellow writers. Unlike many critics, Tallman is worth arguing with.

Moreover, a few of his chosen poets are very striking. Daphne Marlatt is perhaps the most difficult of them, since her language is rich, evocative, and closely textured. She makes a kind of densely packed documentary of the city's seedier side in her *Vancouver Poems* and elsewhere. Sights, movements, sounds abound:

> Alcazar, Cecil, Belmont, New Fountain, names
> stations of the way, to
>
> Entrances
>
>   speak doors that swing under
> *men's, women's (& escorts,* escorted by an era
> gone a little later than the sawdust, smashed glass
> brawls, still, the angry sweep of hand or
> beer-clumsy (weighted, rolling to the floor
>
>   o little man, o little man with dull eyes
> with 3 full glasses at closing time, I take you in.

The poet takes this world in compassionately and imaginatively and then presents it in words that render her sense of the world in herself. This is perhaps a better example of Whitmanesque "proprioception" than is found in the work of some of the other poets, where this notion or method would seem to apply to some poems but not to others.

And, as would be expected, the other especially interesting poets praised by Tallman—George Bowering, bill bissett and John Newlove, who is allowed to be least "proprioceptive"—are also the most individual and least obviously bound to the theory. Bowering, for instance, has great energy and considerable variety. He began as a poet of fact, of Western Canadian history and experience, in a way that placed him in the grand line of Pratt, Birney, and Purdy, about whom he has written a book, but he has developed along esoteric and mystical lines in more recent times in a way that is consistent with his admiration for Margaret Avison. He has also written short fiction, collected in *Flycatcher* and *Protective Footwear,* and two novels, *Mirror on the Floor* and *A Short Sad Book.* So perhaps he will be seen in future to be another of the poet-novelists. But *A Short Sad Book* is more witty monologue than novel and has the effect of Chinese food. It is not substantial enough to remain in the memory. The reader wants more.

As for bill bissett, he is a poet of ecology and Indians, pot and chant—a shaman turning back to the oral tradition. In him the search for ancestors that we find in Purdy involves the overthrow of strict constructions of language, of grammar and syntax and conventional spelling, in order to express a more naked and complete relationship with the environment. He attacks, as do Purdy and Acorn, an American cultural and economic imperialism, "ther one world American horse shit"; he attacks the dominion of mind over flesh and the natural. His experiments in spontaneity, a further development from Purdy's run-on poem, may not always work, and the total rejection of technology, mind and form may be a little naive, but a powerful vision is nevertheless embodied in the flow of his verse.

Similarly, John Newlove, in his more public poems, provides a kind of extension of Purdy's examination of our being here. "Verigin, Moving in Alone," for instance, goes beyond autobiography to a sense of place and prairie and what it was to live there. This exploration goes further in "Ride off Any Horizon" and in "The Pride," Newlove's most ambitious poem, in which he investigates the possibility that we may incorporate the Indians in ourselves as they

> still ride the soil
> in us, dry bones a part
> of the dust in our eyes,
> needed and troubling
> in the glare, in
> our breath, in our
> ears, in our mouths,
> in our bodies entire, in our minds, until at
> last we become them.

This footnote to Purdy's "Remains of an Indian Village" may not be much comfort to the exterminated or surviving Indians. But it conveys the same sense as is found in Purdy's and Atwood's poems, that the past lives on in our imaginative construction of the self, of a national sense of self. Newlove too celebrates a harsh and lovely land, invoking the image of the double-headed snake. He shares the quest of Purdy, Atwood, bissett, Lee, Bowering, Helwig and others: this means that he is much more centrally in the Canadian mainstream than most of the Black Mountain poets. Perhaps that is why he is least proprioceptive.

Both Western and Eastern poets lay stress on openness and flux, the impossibility of fixing things. They have translated the traditional Canadian obsessions with space and ancestors and divergent perspectives on reality into new forms and idioms, some of which owe something to the Black Mountain, but the theology is something of a red herring. All of this contributes to our collective sense of self, a definition that refuses too exact definition. The new poets who have achieved most follow in this way in the footsteps of Purdy and Avison, whether they are influenced by them or not. Such poetry reflects, as did the work of D.C. Scott long ago, the double hook, the balance between beauty and terror that is so appropriate to the Canadian space and, beyond that, in a more general sense, to life on the imperilled earth itself, and also to the ongoing search for a larger Self that comprehends all our regional and racial and other variety.

Canadian poets are quite different from contemporary American or English poets in that they are engaged in the creation of their country. Canadians are, as I wrote in 1969, at "stage of flux in the developing national consciousness roughly comparable to the stage that produced Hawthorne, Melville and Whitman in the United States."

Poet George Jonas and philosopher Lionel Rubinoff have cast some light on the possible nature of our developing consciousness:

> The art of life is compromise, the method of survival is accommodation....
>
> Such people [as Canadians] attempt to create societies that imitate nature's capacity for change and self-repair, instead of artificial, inorganic, mechanical structures that function only in a single direction and for a single purpose without taking into account the multiplicity and flexibility of life....
>
> Life is pliable, moving, wise, fluid and moderate; it resists everything partly and nothing completely; extracts and absorbs the best even from worst; it is easy to deflect but impossible to defeat. It is often said that extremes are militant and moderation is passive, but is there anything more militant than the slow, cautious, conservative force of life?[2]

A group defines itself as a festival of autonomous but interrelated forces. There is no abstract universal destiny, eschatology or essence to which every individual is forced to conform. Thus, for example, in the case of Canada, to be Canadian is, ideally, to celebrate the diversification of forces which hold the nation together.[3]

Perhaps these are expresions of what Canada *should* be. But a movement to communion and community of this kind *is* reflected in Canadian literature. There is in Canadian poets—from Lampman and D.C. Scott to Klein, Purdy and Avison to Atwood and Newlove and others—an essentially religious longing for unity with the world, often seen in terms of the Canadian land but opening out to include the universe, accompanied by an ironic awareness of the diversity of forms and shapes such longing may assume. Dualities of various kinds in our hybrid cultural heritage and development lead to psychological mulitiplicity of perspective. In this respect Canada is and must be a kind of coalition.

Canadian literary themes and forms are no doubt somewhat similar to those of European countries or regions (for example, Russia, Scandinavia) with similar topographical and climatic conditions—Robertson Davies has even suggested, in Donald Cameron's *Conversations with Canadian Novelists*, that the "two great Canadian dramatists are Chekhov and Ibsen"—but those other northern countries have long been settled. Canada has shared only with the United States the experience of engagement with the North American wilderness, and Canadians have been unable for long to think (as the Americans have done) of its "conquest." After the last spike there was still "unhuman emptiness," and Canadians have had to seek accommodation, in every sense. They have had to give themselves up to the world around them, and yet to construct physical and psychological shelters in which to live—some of the time—and survive and grow, to be flexible, to move in and out of the sometimes necessary garrison, to learn female as well as male values. The themes and structures of Canadian poetry have reflected these necessities.

The holy, or "fabled," city is still an ideal of community, not the exaltation of the individual, as Dave Godfrey has observed, and the search for such harmony is complex. This means that a certain kind of ironic or ambivalent tone will accompany technical means that may in themselves be common enough elsewhere. Literature is, after all, international, but the arrangement of the elements will vary according to local circumstance and psychology. Thus Purdy may resemble Whitman in his historic role as national poet, and his technique of utilizing the speaking voice may be comparable to that of the American Beats (Whitman's poetic descendents), but his irony, his uncertainty, his rapid shifts of perspective, his myriad-mindedness, are Canadian. Similarly, Layton is a somewhat more controlled, even more rational prophet than Ginsberg, Atwood a much cooler and more ironic oracle of woman's experience than Sylvia Plath.

And yet, from some more universal perspective, Louis Dudek has written "Everything, whatever it is, is a kind of Canada" ("Canada: Interim Report"). The precise meaning of this is uncertain: possibly it is simply that everything in the cosmos is blank, unrealized, empty; but perhaps it may be that the Canadian possibility and potential is, finally, the human possibility and potential, perhaps even—if this is not too visionary—a phase of evolutionary change for the species at large in the unpredictable future. Not that the urgent and immediate practical problems afford much leisure for possible hubris about Canada's special significance in the larger scheme of things. But it is true that writers working in this space have been inclined to think in terms of large evolutionary and cosmic processes, without ever deluding themselves into thinking that they could direct them. What *is* at least relatively possible is to recognize and be in harmony with them.

Canadians began as cultural half-breeds, as Duncan Campbell Scott intuitively perceived. They had perforce to engage the environment, the outer storm, simply in order to survive. Pratt is the major chronicler of that pioneering even if his traditional form and language are impositions like the "steel syntax" of the railway itself. The modernists introduced an eclecticism of styles and techniques that became—in the hands, especially, of A.M. Klein, Dorothy Livesay, Earle Birney, P.K. Page, and Irving Layton—a vehicle for that "inner weather" of a deeper emotional and intellectual intermingling with our North American place. In the mature work of Al Purdy and Margaret Avison an idiom is developed to express an increasing sense that

> Form has its flow,
> a Heraclitus-river with no riverbank
> we can play poise on now.

> "Intra-Political"

There follows the complementary quest into darkness and openness of the poet-novelists, an exploration that enlarges in another way the sense of life in an open space.

Passing through outer and inner storm, Canadians have refused to be defined too exactly because they have looked on openness and perceived that the void is really a Heraclitean flux in which the glory and the darkness co-exist and balance one another. They have cultivated a shifting, multiple perspective. Both Canada and her poetry are multidimensional, as reality is. I like it that way.

Notes

1. *boundary* 23, no. 1 (1974).
2. George Jonas, "In Praise of Moderation," *Maclean's,* November 1974.
3. Lionel Rubinoff, "Nationalism and Celebration: Reflections on the Sources of Canadian Identity," *Queen's Quarterly* 89 (1975).

INDEX